American Motors

THE LAST INDEPENDENT

Patrick R. Foster

Published by

Krause Publications, Inc.
700 E. State Street
Iola, WI 54990-0001

3 3187 00073 7177

Library of Congress Catalog Number: 92-74792
ISBN: 0-87341-240-0

Printed in the United States of America

338.76

FoS

Contents

Foreword

In the decades prior to World War II, a common term in the automobile industry was "independent automaker." These were the smaller firms, such as Auburn, Hudson, Packard, Willys, and Nash, which served a more focused market than the broader approach used by the "Big Three" makers: Ford, Chrysler and General Motors.

The ranks of the independent makers were decimated by the Great Depression. The surviving makers at the onset of World War II -- Willys/Overland, Hudson, Studebaker, Nash, etc. -- were joined after the war by an upstart new company, Kaiser-Frazer.

This is the story of the longest-lived of the independents. American Motors may seem to have been an unimportant company to some people, but its story is one of importance to industry in general and to the American automotive industry in particular. It is a story of time and travail, success and failure, and perhaps even a fable for modern times. It is enlightening, fascinating and heartbreaking, history at its very best. Read it and enjoy.

A work of this breadth and detail is simply not possible without the help of a great many people. I owe a debt of gratitude to the many ex-AMC people who helped me in this effort, people such as Roy D. Chapin Jr., George Romney, John Conde, William Reddig, Edmund Anderson, the late Richard Teague, Chuck Mashigan, and several others.

Of course, book writing is a lonely career made bearable by friends and family that encourage and give support. My wife, Diane, and daughter, Caitlin, were both supportive and understanding of my long hours away from home while working on this book, and I am grateful for that.

I want to recognize some folks who gave me advice and encouragement throughout the project. Christopher Foster, a fellow writer and historian, served as mentor and one-man support group and has been a great friend as well. Thank you to David Brownell of *Special Interest Autos* magazine for giving me my first break in the business, Leo Carroll for his advice, Bill Wilson for saving my life a few times, and the members of the Society of Automotive Historians, who gave freely of their knowledge and insight. Special thanks to W. Scott Cameron for photographic assistance .

Patricia Klug of Krause Publications deserves special mention for her support of this project as well.

I have always hoped that I would be able to complete a project near and dear to me, an American Motors triology. With this book as the cornerstone, perhaps I will.

Patrick R. Foster
Milford, Connecticut

Chapter 1

1954-1957
A New Corporation,
A New Direction
and a Close Call

The Dance of the Doomed began sometime in 1946; the exact date is hard to fix and is not really important anyway. Like an ancient dinosaur, only vaguely aware that the climate was changing rapidly and it might be time to consider doing something about it, the larger independent automakers in America could sense that a change in their fortunes was coming.

They were all enjoying a robust postwar market, with the pent-up demand of the war years -- 1941-1945 -- unleashing a buying binge in the 1945-1950 period. It had been made doubly sweet by the fact that Detroit had not had to redesign and retool for the postwar boom. Demand was such that the automakers could all offer warmed-over 1940 designs, knowing they would be sold quickly to an eager public.

Of course, this delightfully profitable situation would continue to work only as long as the public continued to buy the existing cars. When the time finally did come to tool new designs, automakers were stunned at the huge expense involved. Postwar inflation had driven the cost of tooling to a level that could only be recovered through price increases, which were held down by competitive pressures; by a large increase in car sales in a newly competitive market; or by better amortization of cost through the sharing of bodies, drivetrains and components with other cars. This need for better amortization became the single most critical business need for the postwar independents.

It was natural that this situation would affect the independents more than the Big Three. General Motors, Ford and Chrysler were all large enough to recover tooling dollars through increased sales and sharing of components with sister divisions. The independents -- Nash, Packard, Hudson,

Willys, Kaiser, and Studebaker -- were stuck. But as long as cars were selling well, few makers bothered to worry about the future, perhaps hoping it would all go on like this forever. As the postwar market began to shift from a seller's market to a buyer's market, the more astute managers in the independent ranks began to cast about for partners.

1954 was the final year for the Nash-Healey, although a few 1954 models were reportedly retitled as 1955s.

And so the dance began, slowly at first, led by reluctant suitors in the game of merger. Packard and Nash held talks in 1946 and again, more seriously, in 1948. Nash approached Hudson with talk of merging. Nash Vice President George Romney, in an internal report written in 1949, stated, "If future merger on any scale is going to be neccessary, merger NOW while companies are financially strong would be the soundest course," and he was right. But the companies instead chose to dance around the issue, wasting precious time. It would cost them dearly later.

It seems that only Nash President George Mason could read the writing on the wall, at least early enough to do something positive. Mason realized, in 1946, that sooner or later the pent-up demand would be sated, and the auto industry would have to get back to a more normal demand, in the meantime facing the new higher cost structures moving into place.

What Mason saw as the solution to the coming shakeout in the industry was a merger of the best of the independents -- Nash, Hudson and Packard -- in a new unified company able to share bodies, engines, and the myriad components that make up a car. This new corporation would have a sales network that could reach from the lower end of the market to the highest price class, and do it while utilizing the economies of scale that its bigger competitors enjoyed. Mason even had a name for this company of the future ... American Motors. Mason approached Packard and Hudson with a firm plan

Nash President George W. Mason initiated merger talks with Packard and later with Hudson.

in 1948.

He was promptly turned down. Packard President Hugh Ferry was insulted by Mason's first offer, and probably believed that the proud and respected Packard Motor Car Company could turn things around. Hudson, too, held out a hope that it could continue as an independent if it increased its share of the market by moving into new niches. And, remember, cars were still selling well.

As the decade of the fifties started moving, the market turned, just as Mason had predicted. The seller's market turned into a buyer's market, and the Big Three began to turn up the heat on its dealers to compete. Hudson, the weakest of the independents, tried to compete by fielding an all-new car in the compact class, where it could avoid selling directly against the Big Three makes. It may have been a sound theory, but the reality of the market was different. The small Hudson, named the Jet, was brought to market for the 1953 model year and was a very costly flop because it not only failed to sell in sufficient quantities, but also used up the bulk of Hudson's new model development budget. The Jet's failure in the market ensured that Hudson would need either a miracle or a merger to continue in the car business.

Packard and Nash, in the meantime, had held exploratory talks on a possible merger. These two

9

The Hudson Jet was dropped from the line-up soon after the formation of American Motors Corporation. A 1953 model is shown here.

companies had much in common, and it is sometimes difficult to understand why they could not agree to a merger. Both manufacturers were well run, having sound financial management that had stood them well in hard times. Both were longtime veterans of the business with good dealer organizations. Both were well respected by the motoring press. And most importantly, from a marketing standpoint, their product lines were complementary, much more so than with the partners they eventually chose.

Perhaps the reluctance to merge was a result of their cash balances, for although hard times were soon to be coming, both Nash and Packard had plenty of cash on hand in 1950. Studebaker and Hudson, in comparison, did not have deep resources to fall back on, and thus were in less of a position to hold out for a better deal than Packard and Nash. And there is just a hint that it may have boiled down to personalities, that the Packard people couldn't see eye to eye with the Nash people.

The new competitive auto market of 1954 sobered everybody pretty quickly. Reality hit like a freight train. It came too fast and too hard, much harder than even Mason had envisioned. A sales war broke out between Ford and Chevrolet, and innocent bystanders like Nash, Packard, Hudson, et all, were caught in the crossfire and suffered an immediate sharp drop in sales. It was a critical time in their histories.

At any rate, history and the market were not going to wait forever, and the old era ended pretty quickly when it happened. Mason, tired of Packard's on-again, off-again attitude and convinced that time had almost run out, reapproached Hudson. Hudson had always been Mason's second choice for its product line competed directly against Nash, its costs were high, and there was little Nash would be able to salvage from Hudson. Perhaps the only two Hudson assets to interest Mason were its dealer body, which could be melded into the Nash structure, and the old Hudson plants, which could

10

be used to build other, non-automotive products or could be liquidated for cash. Still, a merger with a second choice company was better than no merger at all, so Nash approached Hudson once more.

Hudson had been coquettish at earlier proposals, but now, facing huge losses as a result of the Jet's flop in the market and the virtual shutoff of sales of the rest of the line, Hudson was not holding the high cards. A loss of $10.4 million in 1953 had opened its eyes, and the huge drop in auto sales in early 1954 had forced it to the bargaining table, especially as Hudson President A.E. Barrit knew things were going to get worse before they got better. Perhaps a lot worse.

Dated and ponderous: the Hudson Hornet.

To his credit, though, he did right by his stockholders to the end, hammering out a deal to swap Hudson stock for shares in the new company. George Mason, quoted after the negotiations were completed, said, "I have dealt with tough traders before, but this Barrit has a heart of stone." Still, both sides knew they had few other options, and all parties present at the signing of the merger agreement were smiling their best corporate smiles. The merger took place on May 1, 1954, and as George Mason had planned, the merged company was named American Motors.

The details of the merger involved stockholders of Hudson exchanging three shares of Hudson stock for two shares of the more costly Nash stock, while Nash stockholders held onto their existing shares. The corporate name would then be changed to American Motors, and all stockholders would be issued new shares reflecting the name change. The merger proposal listed its book value at $197,793,366 or $34.85 per share for the 5,675,710 shares.

At the time, it was the biggest merger in the history of the automobile business, easily dwarfing the merger of Willys Overland and Kaiser Motors the previous year. George Mason was named chairman of the board, president, chief executive officer, and general manager, while his assistant, George Romney, was named executive vice president. Hudson President Barrit became a director of the company.

George Romney began 1954 as a Nash executive, became executive vice president of the newly formed American Motors Corporation in May, and ended the year as chairman of the board of AMC. Romney was a hard-working executive who neither drank nor smoked.

The new company had 30,000 employees, 55,000 stockholders, 10,000 dealers, and two distinctly different lines of cars that unfortunately competed against each other. They had, as Mason saw it, a narrow time line to integrate their plants, product lines, dealer body, and corporate staffs to compete in the remorseless market that was just then becoming apparent. Mason and Romney set out to try to shape their destiny as best they could.

Mason may have had some faults, namely being loath to delegate responsibility, but when he did delegate it, he usually ended up picking the perfect man for the job. In choosing Romney to be his second in command and heir apparent, Mason had picked a man who was singular in the auto business in those days. Romney had grown up in a family of deeply religious Mormons, was an ex-street preacher for the faith, and had grown to become a man who believed in hard work and dedication to

AMC Design Chief Edmund Anderson.

a cause, a man who knew adversity and skepticism first-hand. In his earlier preaching days, Romney had soapboxed in front of friendless crowds in faraway cities of Europe, trying to convince the wary of his message. The experience would steady him for the hard days that were soon to come to AMC.

Mason had earlier led the effort to begin an in-house design studio for Nash, something rare for an independent automaker. In those days, most independents used the design services of their body suppliers, such as Murray and Budd, or contracted with independent design houses. But in 1950, Mason had approached and hired one of GM's top designers, Edmund E. Anderson, to develop a company design studio, while at the same time hedging his bets by signing a design contract with the then little-known designer, Pininfarina.

Roy D. Chapin Jr., son of one of the founders of Hudson, stayed on board after the merger. Born to wealth, it would have been easy for him to quit the business at this point, but Chapin had been raised on cars and instead took a seat on the board of directors.

Looking at the product position of 1954, it's easy enough to see where the problems lay. The 1954 Hudson line consisted of the Hudson Hornet and Wasp, two similarly sized cars that featured Hudson's famous "Step Down" design. "Step Down" design had been a rage in 1948 when it debuted, but by 1954, having benefited from only minor face-lifting of the body, it looked stale next to the competition. Too, Hudson had missed the boat on the consumer interest in V-8 engines and was able to field only six-cylinder cars, albeit the most powerful and most advanced sixes of their time. The aforementioned Hudson Jet anchored the bottom of the line, and the Jet was a sales disaster.

13

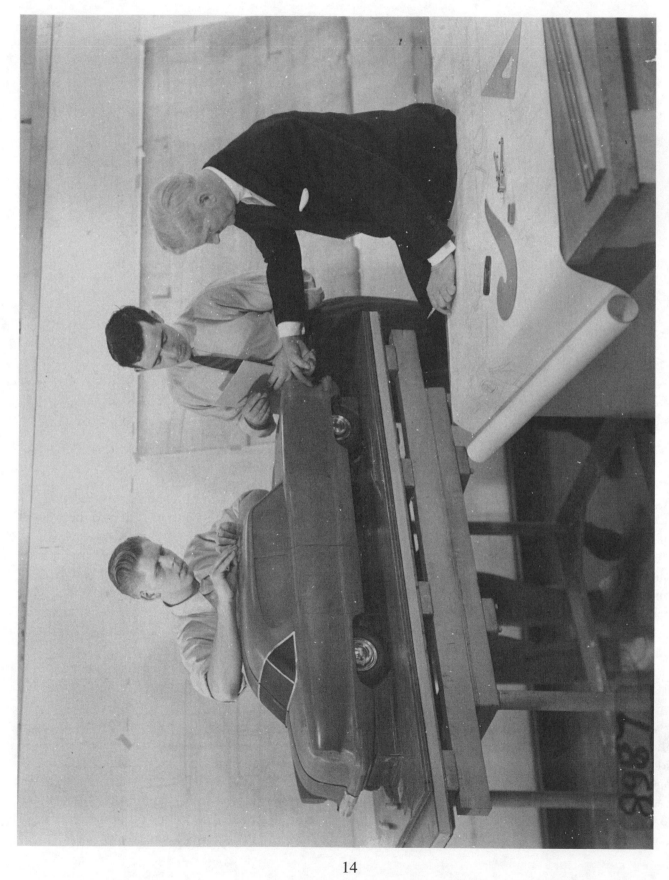

Nash Styling Department, pre-1954. From right: Edmund E. Anderson, Bill Reddig and unidentified modeler.

American Motors styling team. Left to right: Don Stump, interior styling; Don Butler, accessories; Ken Koppet, Hudson studio; Ed Anderson, head of styling; Bill Reddig, assistant to Anderson; and Jack Garnier, Nash studio.

Proposed sports car for 1957-'58, by Jack Garnier.

1954 Nash Rambler Country Club hardtop. Note skirted wheel wells front and rear and Nash hubcaps.

1954 Nash Rambler Custom two-door station wagon.

Nash was better off, productwise, as Nash almost always seemed to be. Its line began with the Metropolitan, a tiny two-door car offered in coupe or convertible and built in England by Austin under contract to Nash. The use of European labor and parts helped keep the Met's price under $1500 while its small size and four-cylinder engine allowed it to achieve gas mileage in the high 30s, quite good for the time. The next step up the scale was the Nash Rambler, available as a two-door sedan, station wagon, convertible and hardtop, all on a 100-inch wheelbase. New this year was a four-door sedan and four-door station wagon on a longer 108-inch wheelbase. Prices began around $1700 for the coupe, but sales were still off in 1954. Further up in size and price were Nash States- man and Ambassador, big, roomy road cars that had been all-new in 1952 and were still attractive enough for the market.

The Nash Statesman competed with the Hudson Wasp in the lower medium price range, while the Hudson Hornet and Ambassador were both in a more expensive price range. The Rambler and the Jet were both compacts, although the Rambler had a price advantage of some importance. This situ- ation of competing against corporate partners would do no good at all, so Mason and Romney, after realizing the competitive disadvantage Hudson had with its dated senior cars and poor-selling Jet, made the decision to consolidate all automaking at the Nash facility in Kenosha, Wisconsin, effec- tive with the start of 1955 production, then only a few months away.

All the old Hudsons were dropped, the seniors because of the dated styling, the Jet because of its high cost and lousy sales. The all-new 1955 Hudsons were based on the existing Nash bodies, but with design features that kept them from appearing too similar. The face-lifting of the Nash senior line to create the Hudson senior line was carried out by Edmund Anderson and his able though little known team of designers. The last Hudson-built Hudson came off the Detroit assembly line on Oct. 29, 1954.

Mason never got to see that last Hudson or share in the marketing of the new 1955 models. In early October 1954, just six months after engineering the merger, Mason fell ill and quite unexpect- edly died. The automotive world was shocked, and the directors of AMC were put in the position of having to replace the single most important man in the organization at short notice. Luckily, Mason had been grooming and training Romney to the degree that the board of directors had faith in his abilities. The day after Mason's funeral, Romney assumed all of Mason's titles and responsibilities.

The 1955 automobiles were already settled, so Romney's first efforts went to the task of consoli- dating the rest of the company. The '55 car lines, while sharing many components and, of course, the bodies, still were distinctive, perhaps more than they should have been.

The 1955 Hudson line again featured Wasp and Hornet names and Hudson's strong six-cylinder engines, only now on a restyled Nash chassis. The new styling was actually an improvement over the dated "Step Down" design, although hard core Hudsonphiles decried the lack of handling precision that came part and parcel with the Nash body. Hudson buyers could now order certain options not available before, such as reclining seats, twin travel beds, and air conditioning.

It seemed to do the trick for 52,688 Hudsons were built in 1955, although a closer look reveals that the bulk of those Hudsons was the new Hudson Rambler. This was a new model made to replace the Jet by simply replacing the Nash badge in the Rambler's grille with a Hudson badge. Still, it was an improvement in overall Hudson sales, albeit one that foreshadowed the coming collapse in con- sumer confidence in the Hudson nameplate.

Over at the Nash side of the business, the 1955 senior cars, the Statesman and Ambassador, car- ried bold front end redesigns which featured in-board headlights. The design was both shocking and very individual, but the series sold at only a moderate rate. As at Hudson, the market was showing interest in the new 108-inch wheelbase Rambler. Although the basic styling was beginning to get a little long in the tooth, the Rambler was a known quantity with a solid reputation for quality and frugality.

Still, things were getting scary. Henry Ford II, grandson of the founder of Ford, started an ongoing price war in 1953 when he vowed an all-out push in 1954 to beat Chevrolet in sales or, as he put it, "kill the company trying." The 1954 price war between Chevy and Ford was the final impetus to form AMC, and it soon pushed Packard into a foolhardy merger with Studebaker. Kaiser had been forced to merge earlier, in 1953, with Willys-Overland, builder of Jeeps. By 1955, Kaiser-Willys announced its intention to abandon the passenger car business in America, concentrating instead on sales of Jeep vehicles. Despite the improvement in plant utilization that had been one of the great hopes of the merger, a nascent American Motors was severely hurt by profit margins that disappeared in the bloody sales war.

At the end of 1955, American Motors reported that it had closed its West Coast plant at El Segundo, California, and later sold it as surplus in 1956. AMC also closed Hudson's main plant, and despite the integration of all auto production at Kenosha (and increased production as well), ended the year with a loss of $6.9 million. And the sales war with the Big Three was not going to end in 1956.*

1955 Rambler Country Club hardtop. Note open front wheel wells, "R" hubcaps and revised grille.

* *Until the 1980 model year, American Motors' fiscal year ran from October through the following September, roughly the same as a typical model year. From 1980 on, AMC used a regular calendar year as its fiscal year.*

1955 Rambler two-door station wagon.

1955 Rambler four-door on the 108-inch wheelbase.

19

1955 Rambler four-door with optional "Fashion-tone" trim and two-tone paint.

It was in late 1954 that Romney made a momentous decision that later proved to be a bold gamble and was somewhat misunderstood. In the dark days of 1954, when sales were going nowhere and profits could not be had, Romney saw that the competition was not going to ease up, and that he could never compete head to head with companies that were 15 times the size of AMC. Although full-size replacements for the Nash and Hudson big cars were being planned, to Romney, one car stood out as perhaps the best choice to bet the farm on, and it was coming down to just that. AMC was losing money, and the cash-draining 1955 sales year wiped out most of the reserves that were left.

Romney was, by 1955, in the unenviable position of having to sell off bits and pieces of the company while trying to formulate a plan to turn things around. One car Anderson was working on was the 1957 Rambler replacement, built on the 108-inch wheelbase chassis. Romney knew he was down to the wire, and would have, at best, enough money to retool only one car. The original plan to retool for a senior line and a new compact line was out the window. AMC's cash position was getting sicker by the day. Faced with the choice, Romney would not have been blamed if he had authorized new big cars. Full-size cars were the mainstay of the market and provided potentially higher margins than compacts.

Mason, for all his foresight, had planned on emphasizing the big Nash and Hudson cars, of course sharing a more cost-effective single chassis/body. But even with that, he would be competing directly against the Big Three automakers. Mason planned to keep the Rambler as a lower-priced compact car, a companion model that could be sold by both dealer organizations. Mason, although a believer in small cars, did not feel the company could survive selling only compact cars. This is where Romney and Mason were fundamentally different. Mason can be said to have been a true small car believer. But Romney was a small car apostle.

Romney knew that his big cars would be competing against the Big Three, any profit margin in them would be squeezed by the competition, and that if unit sales were not high enough, there would be no profits at all, and AMC would be put out of the show.

Against that cold reality, Romney compared the potential of the new car upon which Anderson was working. Anderson's design for the 1957 Rambler retained the 108-inch wheelbase but featured

AMC designer William Reddig was Ed Anderson's assistant. Reddig designed the trademark "dip" in the roofline of the Rambler station wagon and worked on advanced designs for the Metropolitan as well as the landmark 1956 Rambler. Of his assistant, Anderson said, "He was the best -- the very best."

Working on a winner. Standing, left to right: Bill Reddig, Ed Anderson and George Romney. The designer (seated) is unidentified, but the design is the 1956 Rambler.

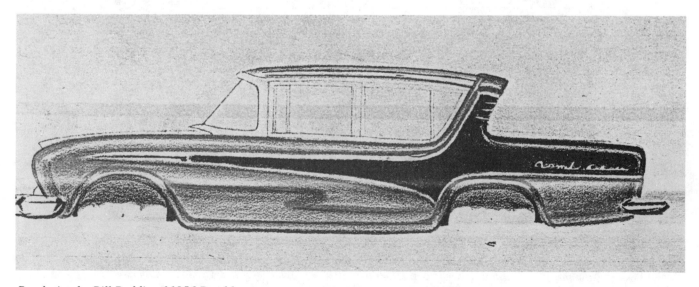

Rendering by Bill Reddig of 1956 Rambler.

22

an all-new body of the modern envelope style, a slab-sided look to replace the rounded look of the '55 models. Rear fenders were lengthened to create the look of a much larger, though still compact, car. Chrome, that staple of the fifties, was used sparingly on the sides, abundantly on the grille. Inset headlights, similar to what the Nash was carrying, were attractive. Anderson designed several two- and three-tone paint schemes, all the rage in that decade, to impress that this was a classy compact.

The design of the body itself was a breakthrough. Anderson designed huge glass areas to give the interior a light, airy effect and to eliminate the claustrophobic feeling so common in small cars of the fifties. The windshield was wraparound, considered a premium feature, as was the rear window. Sitting in the car gave a feeling of being in a slightly smaller, less ostentatious full-sized car, not a low bucks cheap car. Anderson's choice of exterior colors and trims further drove home the point that this was something different. The smaller 100-inch wheelbase two-door was not offered as sales concentrated on the 108-inch wheelbase chassis that seemed to be the size best suited for the family car market.

The problem Romney faced, when he looked over the prototype in 1954, was that he wasn't sure if AMC would still be in business by the time the new car came out for 1957. But he knew he needed that car. It represented a solid entry in the one part of the market where he knew GM, Ford and Chrysler would not be competing in 1956. By aiming for an unrepresented part of the market, AMC would be better able to price the product for the profit it needed, while at the same time offering a style that had no direct competitor. Looking back, there really was only one decision to make, and Romney made it. For 1955, Romney committed the sum of $5 million to advance the 1957 Rambler program to where it could be introduced for the 1956 model year.

Working long hours, Anderson and his team completed the models ahead of schedule. The plant at Kenosha was refitted to build the all-new 1956 Rambler.

Romney was optimistic. In his view, the 1956 Rambler was a unique and all-new car that should sell in big numbers, especially as it would be sold like the 1955 Rambler, by both Nash and Hudson dealers. The 1955 Rambler brochure made no mention of Nash or Hudson, referring to the car only as "The Rambler," but the product itself had been badged according to whichever brand dealer it was sent to. The strategy remained in place for the 1956 Rambler, but it must have been confusing for the average buyer.

Romney himself termed the car a compact, although what he meant was a compact family car versus simply a small car. Today it would be considered an intermediate-sized car.

The 1956 Rambler was very well received by the press. Motor Trend, in an article dated January 1956, noted its improved power, easier entry and exit, larger interior, and manual steering so easy that the test drivers double-checked under the hood to see if it really wasn't power assisted. Other quotes included, "Excellent is the word for the Rambler's brakes" and "Outdistances the old Rambler in every phase of acceleration." Although the new Rambler was not an exciting car, the press generally recognized it as a well-designed, well-built family car with endearing qualities.

Not so with the rest of the American Motors line. The 1956 Hudson and Nash models were still using the body that had appeared on the 1952 Nash. Hailed as one of the most beautiful cars of 1952, the styling had held up well for 1953, 1954 and 1955. But in that decade, newness was the key to the market, and by 1956, the cars were getting stale. The Fords and Chevys had been all new in 1955, the Dodge and Plymouth were new for 1956; even the Packard was new for 1955. The cash crunch at AMC had limited it to redesigning only the Rambler, while the big cars received a series of very low-cost face-lifts. The 1956 Hudson received a new grille and front end trim, a busy mess that was

AMC designer Edmund Anderson.

Compact but spacious -- the 1956 Rambler. Note the wraparound windshield and rear window and smooth fender shapes.

called V-line styling, an attempt to integrate the old Hudson triangle theme with a more modern V (for V-8) theme. It was a reasonable attempt, but lack of funds forced it to be mostly chrome trim and doodads appliqued all over in an attempt to hide the oldish lines of the basic body. It didn't fool too many people, and the big Hudsons sold poorly.

At Nash, it was about the same. The big Nash Ambassador still had the inboard headlights introduced on the 1955 models, and had just new color schemes to show for 1956. Ditto for the Statesman. The line sold better than Hudson, but here again the public was rejecting the senior cars while sales of the new Rambler were hampered by a slow production start-up.

Romney was worried about the results. When 1956 closed out, only 126,575 cars had been wholesaled to dealers and had generated a loss of $19.7 million. Looking closer at the numbers reveals how tough things were, for the operating loss had been $30.4 million, offset by proceeds of $10,662,372 from the sale of one of its subsidiaries, Ranco Incorporated. And the new Rambler actually sold fewer cars than the 1955 model. The rush to get it to market a year early had limited production output.

Still, Romney saw things to encourage him, and he was a man who was easily encouraged. In his "President's Message" in the annual report for 1956, he noted that part of the loss was the cost of moving up the '56 Rambler, and that was a non-recurring $5 million. He also noted that AMC had had to spend extra money, $2.7 million, to move out leftover 1955s and 1956s, and that was also non-recurring, at least hopefully. And he anticipated a reduction in selling and administrative expenses of $7.8 million for 1957.

It had been the belief of Romney and the dealer body that the poor sales of the big Hudsons and Nash were partly caused by the high prices that had to be charged to cover the high cost of the Packard V-8 that had been used since 1955. Romney and Mason had negotiated the purchase of the Packard engines, with attendant Ultramatic transmissions, to meet the market demand for big V-8

25

1956 Hudson Hornet Custom.

26

Not for production: AMC turned down this prototype 1956 Ambassador by Pinin Farina.

1956 Nash Metropolitan hardtop, "the watch charm Rolls-Royce."

1956 Rambler four-door hardtop.

1956 Rambler station wagon. Bill Reddig designed the "dip" in the roofline, necessitated, he said, by a lack of funds to tool a complete roof panel. "I was told to come up with a station wagon roof that could be made from the sedan roof stamping." Thus, only the rear "wagon" stamping was new and welded onto the existing sedan roof.

engines. Neither Nash nor Hudson had a V-8, and while the cost of the Packard unit was high, the agreement called for Packard to purchase components or stampings from AMC in amounts roughly equal to what AMC was spending on power trains.

The problem with the contract was that it did not *require* Packard to buy AMC parts, only to attempt to buy them. Packard did send some bid sheets to AMC, which desperately needed business for its idle Hudson plants, but rejected most of the Hudson bids as too high. Packard never considered having AMC supply body panels or complete bodies, both of which AMC had capacity for and Packard had a need for. In 1954, when Packard purchased its own body plant, an outraged Romney ordered his chief engineer, Meade Moore, to develop an AMC V-8 engine. If Packard would not buy from AMC, then AMC would not buy from Packard.

By April 1956, this new engine was in production. The entire program had cost $10 million, but it produced a suitable V-8 engine for AMC that cost $200 less per engine than the Packard job. And Romney felt sure that a price reduction equal to that on the big eight-cylinder cars would substantially increase their sales in the 1957 model year. So, in April 1956, a new lower-cost model of the Ambassador, called the Special, was introduced. Sales were low, but it was felt that a full year of selling in the 1957 model year would show a dramatic increase.

A limited-production high-performance Rambler, equipped with the new 327 cid V-8, was planned as a flashy addition to the 1957 line. It was to be called the Rambler Rebel.

1957 Rambler Rebel. This limited production car was equipped with the 327 cid V-8. It was supposed to be fuel-injected but problems with the injection system meant most, if not all, came carbureted. Regardless, this was a barnstormer.

So Romney ended 1956 on a hopeful note. As he noted in a very moving and dramatic speech made to his dealers, a sales increase of just 30,000 units would produce a profit for 1957. This was certainly doable with the all-new Rambler, new V-8 engine, lower-priced Nash and Hudson models, and the popular Metropolitan. All it took was for everyone to do his or her best, work hard, keep an eye on costs, and most important, keep the company afloat long enough to see the coming recovery. 1957 was going to be better. 1957 was going to be the year American Motors came into its own.

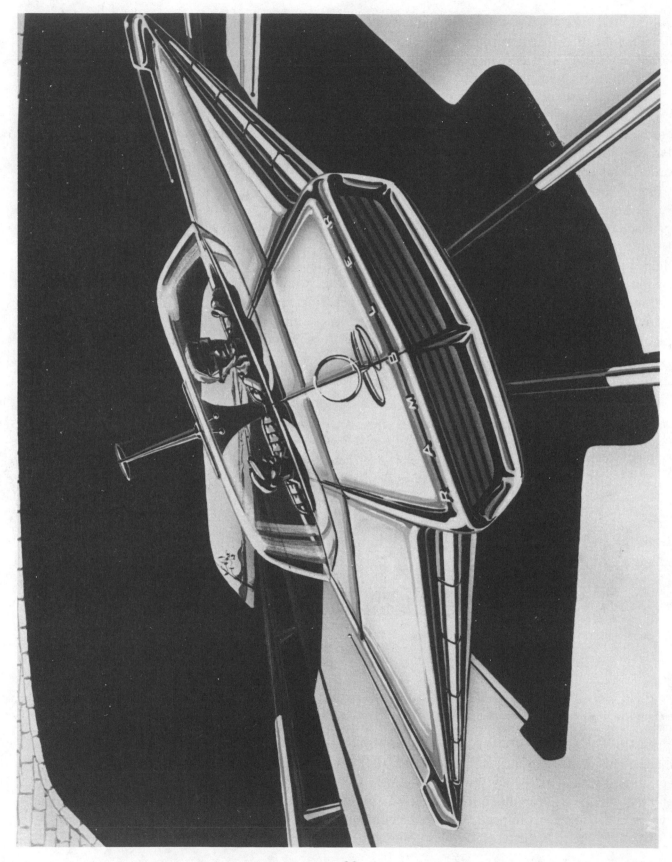

Purely for fun, the Rambler "Rail-Car" design by Bill Reddig evolved from an earlier sketch.

1957 Rambler four-door sedan and station wagon. Only slight changes were made to the front end.

One year later, American Motors summed up 1957 in its annual report to the stockholders this way: "Operations of the Corporation and its consolidated subsidiaries for the 1957 fiscal year showed net sales of $362,234,208 compared with $408,407,637 in 1956. The 1957 net operating loss of $10,533,200, plus a provision of $1,300,000 for revaluation of idle property held for sale, resulted in a loss for the year of $11,833,200."

Another losing year, and on the surface, worse than the prior year. Wholesale sales of 119,586 cars were down from even the year before. Yet, when the 1957 model year ended, American Motors was more confident than ever about its future. The reasons were all sensible, if you knew where to look and could decipher them correctly. The reduction in unit sales had been entirely in the Hudson/Nash senior lines. Sales of the Rambler had been 90,155, compared with just 75,147 in 1956. The sales increase had begun in the spring of '57, and for May and June, Rambler scored its two best sales months ever up to that time. The car was catching on with the public, and the press was happy to go along for the ride. Numerous articles appeared in daily papers touting the advantages of the compact.

1957 Rambler four-door hardtop.

The Rambler was coming into its own just as Hudson and Nash big cars were collapsing in the market. Unit sales of the two senior lines were poor in 1956, and for 1957 they dropped even further.

Now for 1958, Ed Anderson came up with a low-cost reskinning of the basic Rambler that retained all its sturdy virtues while endowing it with wonderfully newer styling. Gone were the rounded fenders and inset headlights, replaced now by flatter, crisper fenders and fender-mounted quad headlamps, a styling feature that was all the rage in 1958.

Never before seen photo of the experimental slide-down rear window. This was built into a production 1956 Rambler and was planned for 1958 production, but was never put into production. Designer Ed Anderson bought this prototype for his own use.

Rendering by Bill Reddig of proposed Rambler two-door hardtop.

From 1955-1958, Bill Reddig drew far-out ideas for future Metropolitans.

Romney had also seen the end of the line in sales of Nash and Hudson brands in 1957, when their sales dribbled to less than 10,000. Romney had declared to his dealers, in 1956, that the 1958 model lineup would include both Hudson and Nash models. Indeed, the decision to discontinue the two brands wasn't made until just before the start-up of 1958 production, so strong was the feeling of loyalty. But in the end there was only one decision to make, and Romney made it. There was no money to tool up a new line of senior cars. Anderson came up with what he called the Hudson Rebel by using a Rambler chassis stretched to a 117-inch wheelbase, using the new 1958 body lines and unique Hudson trim. A similar proposal for the 1958 Nash carried the Nash Ambassador nameplate. But Romney knew that his marketing efforts were being hampered by product confusion over the use of Nash and Hudson nameplates for identical cars, and further, that the Rambler product could stand on its own merits, would, in fact, probably do better in the market without the extra baggage of the Hudson/Nash names attached. The Rambler was earning a reputation as a value car, and its high

34

This styling mock-up of a proposed "Hudson Rebel" used 1958 Rambler styling on a stretched 117-inch wheelbase. This proposal eventually became the production 1958 Ambassador by Rambler.

Proposed 1958 Nash Ambassador. Note the different fender emblems.

Two views of the proposed 1958 Hudson.

Designer Jack Garnier proposed this two-door sports coupe.

resale value was becomming a marketing tool. Romney knew that, for 1958, his best bet was to, as he put it, "sink or swim with the Rambler."

And so, as he ended 1957 with a loss, Romney looked once again to next year as the one of salvation. American Motors' cash balance at the end of fiscal 1957 stood at a mere $22.6 million dollars, down from $26.5 million in 1956, so things would have to get better soon.

Chapter 2

1958-1963
The Glory Years

The year 1958 should not have held out much hope for the struggling American Motors Corporation. True, it did have a restyled Rambler to show, and the prior year's Rambler sales had been on an upswing. But a cynical person, and there were many in 1958, would point out that the new Rambler would be struggling to continue to establish itself in a down market, a real bear market that reflected the so-called "Eisenhower Recession." And it was a terrible year for the car makers. The medium and high price makes -- Mercury, Olds, Pontiac, etc. -- were hard hit by a huge drop in unit sales. Nash and Hudson cars were gone, ended with the pathetic trickle of 1957 models that had been sold. The dealer body had been upset when they heard the news, but by mid-1958, it was looking to be one of the smarter moves AMC had made. Medium cars of all makes were a drug on the market, and the tired-looking Hudson/Nash duet would not have sold at all.

But anyone waiting with a shovel to bury American Motors got a surprise, for 1958 was, at last and finally, **the year**. 1958 was the turning point in the corporation's fortunes when all the cost cutting, consolidation, model trimming, plant closings and layoffs, combined with handsome restyling by Anderson and a more aggressive and more confident dealer body, produced the long-awaited turnaround.

The 1958 lineup was strong. The big seller was what Romney had always predicted would be what he called a "basic volume car," the 1958 Rambler on the 108-inch wheelbase. It came in a range of four-door sedans, four-door hardtops, and four-door stationwagons in both Rambler six-cylinder and Rambler Rebel V-8 models. The Rebel now used a more pedestrian 250 cid V-8, but with a four- barrel carburetor and solid lifters, it still had spunk and put out 215 horsepower. The Rambler six-cylinder had the time-tested 195.6 cid cast iron overhead valve engine. The standard six-cylinder car was sometimes referred to as the Rambler Economy Six. The new top-of-the-line

38

Left to right: Edmund Anderson; Meade Moore, vehicle engineering; Roy D. Chapin, executive vice president; Elmer Bernitt, vice president - automotive operations; and Bill Reddig.

Design sketch by Bill Reddig for possible family van.

Top: The 1958 Rambler Rebel V-8 station wagon. Bottom: 1958 Rambler Rebel V-8 sedan.

RODUCING THE DISTINGUISHED *Ambassador*

Station Wagon Family

HARDTOP CROSS COUNTRY

1958 Ambassador.

car for AMC was the Ambassador, which was not marketed as the Rambler Ambassador, but as the "Ambassador by Rambler." This gave it distinction from the lower-priced cars, which it resembled, while permitting it to serve as a sort of spiritual replacement for the former Nash and Hudson senior cars. The Ambassador, for all that, looked like the Ramblers but with a much longer front end, the result of the wheelbase having been increased to 117 inches. The Ambassador grille was a bit more fussy, the trademark Ambassador emblems were present on the wheelcovers and, of course, the interior trim was much improved. Still, the uninitiated would be hard-pressed to tell one from the other. Of course, the Ambassadors received a bigger engine than the Ramblers: AMC's modern 327 cid cast iron V-8. The top of the Ambassador lineup was a body style that was unique to American Motors, one that had made its debut on the 1956 Rambler but for 1958 would be offered only on AMC's most costly car. The 1958 Ambassador four-door hardtop station wagon, available only in expensive Custom trim, was certainly an eye catcher, unlike anything else on the road, and perhaps the only time a station wagon served as the prestige car in a maker's lineup.

A surprise addition to the lineup appeared in January 1958 when the old 100-inch wheelbase Rambler returned to the showrooms as the Rambler American, in one instant returning a popular style and introducing what would become the most famous Rambler nameplate.

Its return had been decided by Romney, who knew that in any sales situation a company had to

41

offer a range of models, if for no other reason than to give the customer a choice. He also realized that a very low priced car would be a good draw to his showrooms, where the customer might buy that car or decide to move up a bit to the more expensive (and profitable) 108-inch wheelbase Ramblers. Romney was a smart trader and a frugal one as well, and realizing that AMC did not have the cash available to engineer a completely new companion car, he decided to bring back the old 100-inch wheelbase Rambler to provide an entry level automobile to the public. It's important to remember at this point that AMC already had the Metropolitan at the bottom of its lineup, but Romney and his team knew that the American size of the small Rambler would appeal to a wider segment of the market than the Met was getting. Unlike the Metropolitan, this small car would be badged as a Rambler.

Reliable Ed Anderson had been put on the job of changing enough of the old car to make it look new without running up any tooling bills in the process, a nearly impossible job that Anderson accomplished neatly and quickly. The old Rambler's front wheel openings, previously enclosed as an aerodynamic styling trademark, were opened up per Romney's orders for the 1955 model year. Now, Anderson opened up the rear wheel wells, creating a much more contemporary look. The hood line had been lowered, too, but Anderson's stylists now replaced the egg crate grille with one of fine mesh. Trim was simplified with a narrow chrome strip running along the top of the doors and down the beltline to effect a slightly lower look. The old two-door hardtop and convertible styles were

Although it had been dropped at the end of the 1955 model year, the 100-inch wheelbase Rambler returned as the Rambler American for 1958. Note the opened-up rear wheel wells, fine mesh grille and chrome strip running along the belt line.

deemed too old fashioned (and expensive to build) and were dropped from the line. The American for l958 was offered only in a low-priced two-door sedan in two trim levels, Super and Deluxe.

The Metropolitan was still in the lineup, it being a low-investment, fairly high-selling import that had escaped the fate of its other import cousins, the Nash-Healey and Hudson Italia. For 1958, the Met had no significant changes as attention was fixed on the volume cars.

Designer Bill Reddig worked up a couple of prototype Metropolitan station wagons, handsome and practical cars, but management decided the tooling expense would push the small car's price to a level that the public wouldn't bear, so they were never put into production. They had potential to substantially increase Met sales. At least one of the prototypes still exists.

The press had been warming to AMC for a couple years, cheering it on as the underdog and getting on the bandwagon as the public began to consider the compact car. When Motor Trend tested the 1958 Rambler, it gave praise for "all new styling, increased power with a bit more fuel economy ... better driver's position and greatly improved interior." In one of the few instances for any magazine, Motor Trend credited Anderson for his restyling efforts. Generally, Anderson was unknown to the press. Motor Life, in a November 1957 article, also praised the styling, saying, "The new treatment is much crisper and cleaner than before." The quad headlamps came in for much praise as they were a new styling feature in America and were generally seen in more expensive cars. American Motors' sales success had started to ramp up in May 1957, so when the '58s came out some five months later, the industry held its breath, waiting to see if the face-lifted cars would continue to grow in the market or if it had all been a short-lived fluke.

They needn't have worried, for when Romney closed the model year out, 1958 ended in the black, the first time American Motors showed a full year profit. Wholesale sales of 189,807 cars were reported, the profit came in at just over $26 million, and because of the tax loss carryforwards from the prior years, it was all tax free. Of the total cars sold, 42,196 had been the new Rambler American, successful despite its late entry into the market. The new Ambassador had sold in smaller numbers, and the flashy Ambassador hardtop station wagon found just 294 buyers. America was in a recession and the glitzier models were shunned by value shoppers.

The sales success worked like a tonic on the company. Employees went to work wearing small pins provided by Romney that said "LBC," meaning "Let's Be Competitive," but insiders claimed it really meant "Let's Beat Chevrolet." The entire management felt a new confidence, and thus invigorated, set out to build on the sales momentum of 1958. The Metropolitan was revamped for the 1959 battle, receiving, finally, an outside opening trunk lid, vent windows, bigger tires, and adjustable front seat. The Rambler American lineup was enlarged by the addition of a new two-door station wagon model, the result of a flood of requests by old line customers to reintroduce what had always been a popular model at Nash. The range still came in two trim levels, Deluxe and Super, all on the 100-inch wheelbase.

For 1959, AMC held steady with the styling of the Rambler Six and Rebel V-8 models and added refinements to them. Newly available were individually adjustable front seats and headrests (an industry first), dual exhausts, and revised trim. The grille was slightly different on both Rambler Six and Rambler Rebel V-8 as well as on the Ambassador.

Romney had always hoped for a "basic volume" car line, and now he had two, for the American sold better than expected in 1958 and it would almost certainly do better in 1959, and, of course, the mainline 108-inch wheelbase Ramblers would be the big volume make. The decision had been made to increase production substantially to take advantage of the expected increase in deliveries.

At the beginning of 1958, designer William Reddig, left, was manager of exterior styling for AMC. Reddig was later promoted to head Kelvinator appliance design. At right is AMC Director of Styling Edmund E. Anderson. Note the large fins on the clay model.

1959 Ambassador four-door hardtop shows refined side trim.

For 1959, the Rambler American added this two-door station wagon, on the 100-inch wheelbase, to its lineup. An interesting note is the house in the background - it belonged to styling chief Ed Anderson.

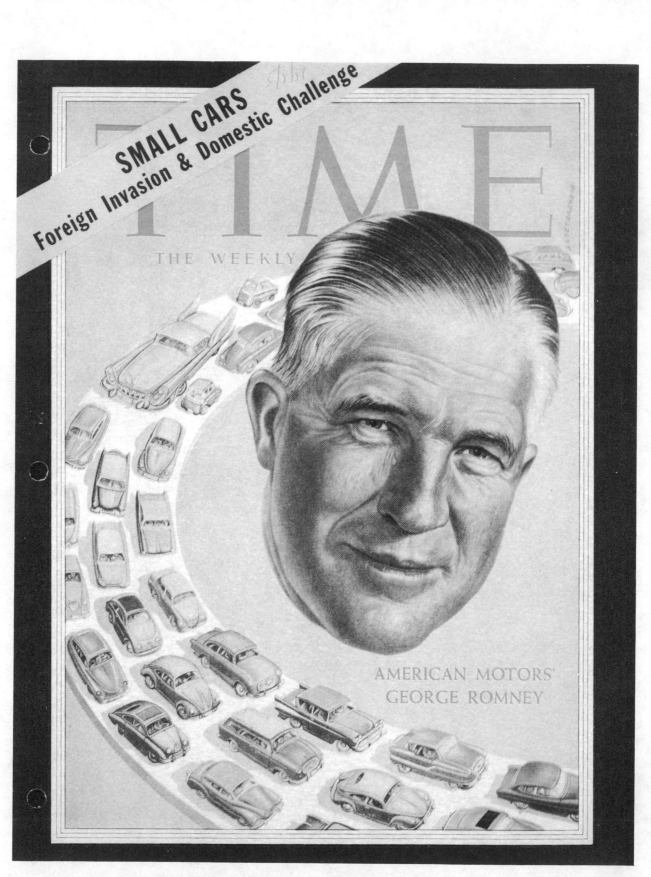

*The April 6, 1959 issue of **Time** magazine featured George Romney.*

The company had a lot of help in getting its sales pitch to the public, for in 1959, the Rambler was the darling of the press, one of the few makes to have increased sales in 1958 and now rolling like a juggernaut in the market. In November 1958, Rambler bragged that it had outproduced Pontiac for the year, and the 1959 schedule would be much more frantic.

And frantic it was, for AMC wholesaled 386,414 cars worldwide in 1959. It was a record, the highest sales ever achieved by an independent. Of the total, a surprising 16,956 were the Metropolitan, showing renewed strength despite its somewhat dated styling and lack of an automatic transmission. The American had gone to a new high with over 90,000 units delivered.

The 1959 Rambler featured a pleasant face lift.

Sales of the Ambassador continued to be low, but the volume achieved by the Rambler Six and Rebel V-8 was both gratifying and profitable. Because the bulk of the amortization costs were already paid on the cars, profits soared along with sales, reaching just over $60 million.

This success came in a year when Studebaker had introduced its new Lark, a car similar in concept to the 108-inch Rambler in that it was marketed as a smaller, family-sized car rather than a small compact like the American. Despite competition from the new Lark, the carryover lineup of Ramblers had captured the imagination of the public and had accelerated its position in the market. Romney, of course, was pleased, but he knew he had to keep up the momentum, for the Rambler was on a roll that had to continue so money could be provided for a host of projects that had been placed on the back burner when cash was tight. First priority was to enlarge and modernize the Kenosha, Wisconsin main plant, a plant that had been a part of Nash, and before that, in the early days of the century, the Jeffery assembly plant. The building itself was all right, but the assembly line needed more modern tools to keep pace with expanded production. The engine assembly line needed modernizing as well. Further production was needed to handle the anticipated increase in U.S. sales as well as overseas sales, where there was a renewed effort to sell the Rambler.

1959 Ambassador hardtop station wagon. Note the new grille design.

Pretty and powerful, the 1959 Rambler Rebel V-8.

The sales success had to continue into 1960 and beyond, but Romney was convinced the corporation had turned the corner, just as he was convinced that the reason was because of the inherent value of the compact car. He planned to continue to pitch the compact car philosophy in 1960 and maintain a close watch on business costs, especially the cost of tooling.

1959 Rambler Rebel four-door sedan.

1959 Rambler Rebel station wagon.

Romney was featured in the sales catalogs that year, where he explained the reasons for the success of the 1959 models and pronounced the 1960 Ramblers "The New Standard of Basic Excellence." He further stated the Rambler "... offers even greater economy -- smooth trouble-free performance ... highest resale value." He was right on all points, especially on resale value. Contrary to popular belief, the Rambler, even the early fifties models, had always held onto their value better than most cars. It was partly because they had succeeded in the market. The Willys Aero, Hudson Jet, and Henry J all were slow sellers as used cars because they had been slow sellers in the new car showrooms. Not so the Rambler, and since 1956 it had been one of the top cars in resale value retained.

The 1958s and 1959s sold well, so the decision was made to retain the basic Rambler chassis and do a mild reskinning of the outside, enough to make it appear new but not enough to scare away anyone interested in buying one. Edmund Anderson, with able assistant Bill Reddig, restyled the rear fenders to reduce but not eliminate the fins. Anderson, thinking like the ex-GM man that he was, realized that to drop the fins abruptly would be an admission of lack of faith in a design concept the public had once loved and still liked, sort of. Like the concurrent Chevrolet, the Rambler's fins were reduced in size and canted to the side to give a newer look. The basic body shell was retained with the now trademark reverse sweep C pillar and mild wraparound windshield, but the front end was given a more pleasing look. The hood ornaments were gone; the grille was new with a square, more integrated look. The side trim was revised as well -- less curvy than before and perhaps a bit plainer. The popular two-tone paint schemes were plainer, too, with the body usually one solid color and the roof a separate contrasting color.

In those days, air conditioning was still a fairly rare option, so white was a popular choice for the roof color to help keep the interior cool. The Ambassador was freshened in a similar manner, but

The 1960 Ambassador four-door hardtop shows off new rear design.

50

The 1960 Ambassador four-door hardtop station wagon. Note smaller fins, revised side trim and grille.

1960 Rambler station wagon.

still riding on the 117-inch wheelbase. The 1960 auto market was not an outstanding one, but the Ramblers still sold well. By the end of the fiscal year, American Motors reported wholesale sales of 478,249 cars worldwide and a profit of $48,243,361. Dollar sales volume for the corporation passed the $1 billion mark for the first time, at $1,057,716,447. Things were really happening.

In the 1960 annual report to the stockholders, a smiling Romney, pictured in shirtsleeves at his desk with two phones and a pile of paperwork for company, radiated confidence. In his "President's Letter," he noted that Rambler production capacity had been more than doubled, and that cost efficiencies were expected to result from the transition of production from overtime to straight time on the newly expanded lines.

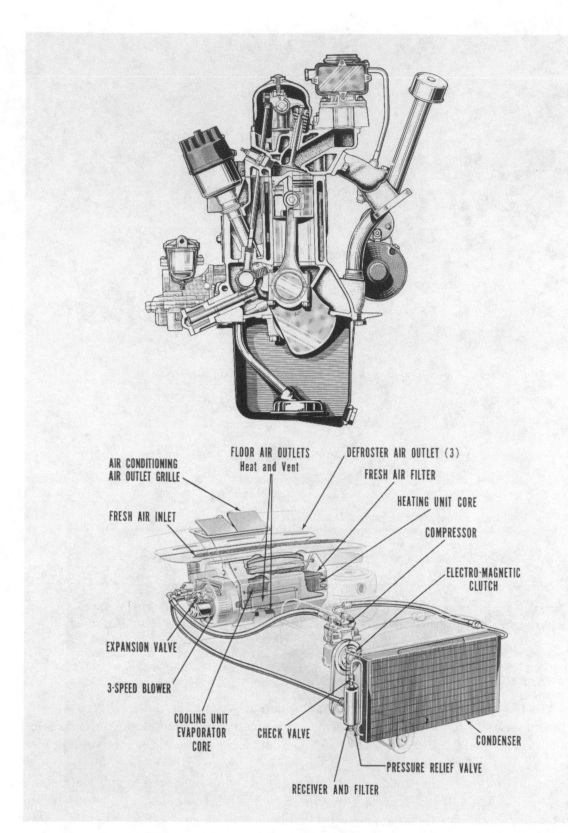

AIR CONDITIONING
AIR OUTLET GRILLE

FLOOR AIR OUTLETS
Heat and Vent

DEFROSTER AIR OUTLET (3)

FRESH AIR FILTER

HEATING UNIT CORE

COMPRESSOR

ELECTRO-MAGNETIC
CLUTCH

FRESH AIR INLET

EXPANSION VALVE

3-SPEED BLOWER

COOLING UNIT
EVAPORATOR
CORE

CHECK VALVE

CONDENSER

PRESSURE RELIEF VALVE

RECEIVER AND FILTER

Top: "The old reliable" Rambler 195.6 cid six. Bottom: The 1960 version of Rambler's "All-Season" air conditioning featured a new aluminum compressor that reduced weight by 19 pounds.

52

1960 Rambler four-door sedan. This year, the tailfins were smaller and canted to one side.

Romney had good reason to smile as the Rambler was having its fourth straight year of sales increases. Additionally, Romney had been recognized as the man who had turned the trick, had kept the company together during the dark days of 1954-1957, and had successfully merged the two old car companies into one new solid whole, a company that was now poised to do what was considered impossible ... make a run for a spot in the "low-priced three": Chevy, Ford, and Plymouth. The low-priced three had been the traditional biggest sellers, the basic volume cars of their respective companies. To grab hold of third place would take a lot of doing, including kicking Plymouth out of its jealously held spot.

Romney also announced plans to again assemble Ramblers in Canada, beginning in January 1961. The previous AMC plant in Canada had been sold in a retrenchment move during the hard times of 1957, but mounting demand forced AMC to buy a newer plant in Brampton, Ontario. The new plant deal was a sweetheart, engineered by a smooth-talking Roy Chapin. The whole thing amounted to a swap of AMC land for the Brampton building, which resulted in a better factory at no cost to the company, save the expense of tooling it. Contracts were signed to begin assembly of Ramblers in Malta and Australia as well. The overseas operations were beginning to contribute very good volume to the company.

A surface glance at the numbers reveals a well-run corporation, deep in an expansion and earning handsome profits. Below that surface were changes and challenges. The most noticeable was the drop in earnings that occurred. Although sales had increased $188,000,000, net profits had dropped from $60 million to $48 million. Now, as Romney pointed out, 1959s profits had benefited from a tax loss carryforward that had, in essence, saved the company $12 million. The gross profit for both years had been $105 million, but the tax loss carryforwards were used by 1960, so taxes of $57 mil-

53

Top: Rambler's all-welded single-unit construction. Bottom: Rambler "Deep coil" front suspension.

In approximately 1958, designer Bill Reddig sketched this idea for a redesign of the American. This is very close to the actual 1961 car.

For a 1961 auto show, this special Metropolitan convertible, with unique trim, was shown.

One of Bill Reddig's last automobile drawings was this small van-type vehicle.

lion had reduced the net take-home to $48 million. What was worrysome was that the gross profit of $105 million had come from over $1 billion in sales in 1960 versus just $869 million in 1959. Thus, the profit margin was lower in 1960. That had come as a result of a $31 million expenditure in tooling to expand Kenosha's output to 600,000 cars per year, making it the largest single auto plant in the country. The increased costs also came from a newly expanded workforce, which increased from 1959's 25,372 to 30,255 in 1960. The payroll was growing and each person on it was better paid than in prior years. It was not a large problem now when sales were hot, but it could prove troublesome if sales dropped much.

In Detroit, at the American Motors headquarters building, Ed Anderson and crew were extremely busy working on future products for AMC. It was felt that the Farina-styled Rambler American was due for a restyling as its fifties look was dated and could not be expected to hold up for long in the new decade. Work was just starting on what would be the first completely new Ramblers in eight years, the all-new line planned for 1963. Designers were sketching ideas for a new Metropolitan for 1962 to come out one year after the reskinned American for 1961.

Anderson was understandably overworked, a situation made worse when his assistant, Bill Reddig, was reassigned and promoted to head the design staff at the Kelvinator Appliance Division. The loss for Anderson was twofold, for Reddig was a very talented designer and a close friend. Since Anderson had lost his larynx earlier to cancer, his speech was strained and harsh. Many times in the past, as he struggled to make himself understood to others, sometimes redfaced and sweating at the effort, Reddig had stepped in to speak for Ed, helping his boss be understood. Many in the company at that time referred to Reddig as "Ed Anderson's voice."

For Anderson there was a question of titles. An old line company man, Anderson had swallowed hard and pocketed his pride in the early fifties when Pininfarina had been given credit for the highly acclaimed 1952 Nash and other designs that Anderson had actually done. The Nash sales department had decided that Pininfarina was a more glamourous name to use in advertising, and Ed went along with the charade. But what he wanted now in 1960 was what his contemporaries at the Big Three had, which was the title of vice president of styling. It would give him a measure of prestige that he had given up before and now deserved more than ever. More importantly, it would remove him from being an employee of the engineering department, where he had few allies. Anderson was constantly fighting staffing cuts and program reductions as the engineering department fought some of his more radical projects.

Also occurring in this time frame was the emergence of Roy Abernethy as a man to be reckoned with. Abernethy had been George Mason's choice for sales manager for AMC, and Romney hired him just before Mason died. Abernethy came from Willys, by way of Kaiser Frazer, and had done a good job keeping the dealer body together during the rough days and moving it all out during the past few years.

Design chief Ed Anderson with unidentified woman, chosing interior fabrics for the 1961 Ramblers.

The company itself was spending money at a fast clip, tooling for higher and higher production levels. A total of $31,000,000 had been spent at Kenosha to increase output. The profit of 1960 had certainly been lessened by that expenditure. A prototype of an advanced lightweight jeep-type vehicle, called the Mighty Mite, had been purchased from an independent designer, along with all rights to the design, and efforts were being made to procure a contract from the military to build the vehicle in quantity.

Certainly the darkest cloud on the horizon was Romney himself, or rather, Romney's future plans. Bitten by the politics bug, Romney began to explore the idea of running for governor of Michigan. What this might do to AMC was an unknown, but for the moment it seemed that the AMC comeback was so solid that nothing could derail it. What no one seemed to realize at this point was the depth of Ed Anderson's dissatisfaction and that it was coming at the same time that Romney was making plans to leave the company. In 1960, Chevy was introducing its new small car wonder, the Corvair, with a 108-inch wheelbase like the Rambler. Worse yet, Ford had a very nice small car called the Falcon that was setting sales records, while Chrysler was pitching small cars with its Plymouth Valiant. Studebaker was still in there swinging with the Lark, while the little Volkswagen was a hot-selling foreigner with which Americans were falling in love. The market was getting crowded, and it didn't look like the sort of market in which to break in a new management team.

As the market started to get crowded in the compact end, AMC was redesigning its core products. The American had sold well in 1958, 1959 and 1960, but it was clear that a new style would be needed soon. Some in the company argued for a complete redesign, but in the end a more complex program was decided upon. Product Planning and Styling had agreed on a program to integrate the basic chassis of all AMC products onto one basic platform to effect the maximum savings on tooling costs. As the plan worked out, the Rambler Classic and Rambler Ambassador would share an all-new and longer 112-inch wheelbase chassis. The Rambler American would also use this basic chassis, shortened to 106 inches and narrowed to reduce material costs. The American two-door could share its doors with the Classic/Ambassador. Inner body panels, such as wheelhousings, were unseen and could also be shared. It would, as Romney said, "allow us to price the American very close to the Volkswagen, and, of course, the Rambler was much more of a car." The target dates for introduction were fall of 1962 for the Classic/Ambassador and fall of 1963 for the American.

The problem was that a new American was needed sooner, by the fall of 1960. So Romney, frugal man that he was, ordered Anderson to reskin the existing American for the 1961 model year. What he wanted was simple enough: a completely restyled car that would be more modern than the existing car, would maintain a family resemblance with the current line of big Ramblers, and be handsome enough to sell in volume. The real trick, though, was that it had to be done using the inner body panels of the existing American, a body shell that dated back to 1950! Romney, realizing that the primary appeal of the American was its low price, wanted to do the new car cheaply by reusing the inner body panel tooling. Thus, he budgeted only enough money to restyle (or face-lift) the body panels.

Anderson, however, came up with a real beauty, a jewel of a small car. The 1961 Rambler American looked new from every angle. In a sharp contrast with design practice of that era, the new American was more compact than ever before, some five inches shorter overall and four inches narrower. Interior room was identical to the prior years because the inner stampings were a carryover. The beltline was a little tall for the time, a result again of the carryover body shell, but it really wasn't too much higher than the Ford and Chevy offerings. To inject some excitement into the line,

Ed Anderson's clever face lift of the 1960 Rambler American resulted in this pert and pretty 1961 American convertible.

Although all previous Rambler four-door station wagons had been built on the 108-inch or larger wheelbase, for 1961 Ed Anderson designed this useful four-door wagon on a 100-inch wheelbase.

Appearing all new, the 1961 American was really just a very clever reskin.

Anderson created a convertible model -- a real convertible without the roof rails that the earlier Nash Ramblers had worn. A four-door sedan and four-door station wagon were in the lineup, an easy task since a four-door sedan on the 100-inch wheelbase had debuted on the 1960 line. And two-door sedans and a low price two-door station wagon rounded out the very complete selection. The time-honored 195.6 cid cast iron six with L head was still standard equipment, but an overhead valve version was also available, either as standard equipment on the higher priced models or as an option on the lesser series.

The 1961 Rambler Six was now called the Rambler Classic Six, while the Rambler Rebel was renamed the Rambler Classic V-8. The volume model, the Classic Six, now offered a die cast aluminum block version of the 195.6 cid engine, a product move with which the industry was experimenting. Styling changes on the Classics were small but noticeable. The front fenders were new, slightly more compact than before, and the headlights were moved to the grille opening in a semi free-floating fashion. The grille itself was of finer mesh and had the trademark Rambler lettering below the grille instead of atop it. The hood was new, lower and more subtly sculpted than before. The hood front and fender tops formed an eyebrow look that is quite handsome when studied in detail. The surface development and care taken with highlighting and shadows shows the General Motors experience of Anderson, although by now he had been gone from GM for about 10 years.

The big Rambler was changing each year, but slowly, subtly, so that each preceding year's car was not instantly obsoleted; each new year showed a touch of newness, a hint of something different, enough so the public could see the changes without being scared away by them.

61

The American Motors exhibit at the Chicago Auto Show. Ed Anderson bought this white on white 1961 American convertible for his wife.

Designer Ed Anderson, his wife and the 1961 Rambler American.

1961 Rambler Classic station wagon shows off its restyled front end and "eyebrow" front fenders. Note the family resemblance to the 1961 American.

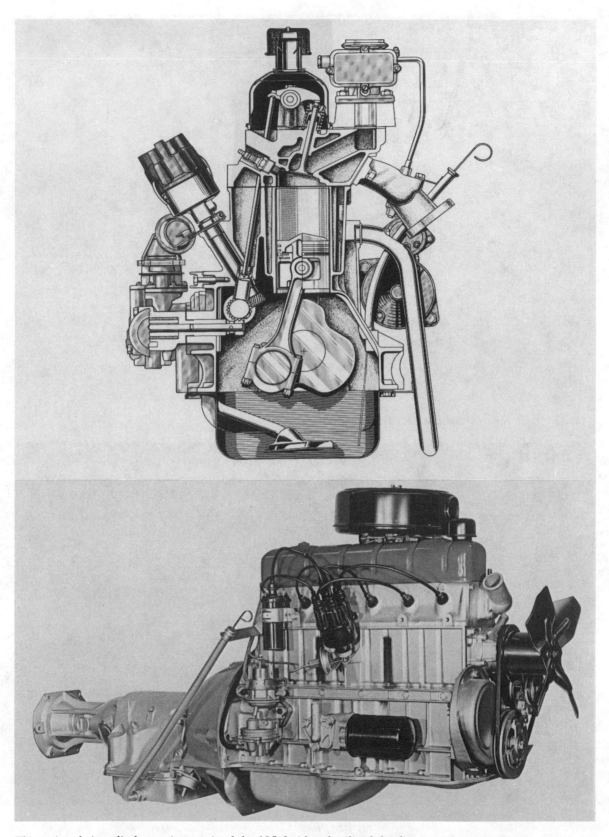

The optional six-cylinder engine retained the 195.6 cid and utilized the die-case aluminum block.

The 1961 Ambassador was something else again. Still riding on the 117-inch wheelbase, the Ambassador featured a front end restyle that was almost out of this world. Like the Classic, the Ambassador got a new hood, but this one was even lower and sculpted with a pronounced dip in the center. The headlights were also moved to the grille area, but the grille itself was narrowed and shaped like an inverted keystone, with straight section ribs and the Ambassador nameplate in large script. The headlights were mounted in four pods that gave a more pronounced free-standing look, and the front fenders were scalloped to help blend it all in with the rest of the (carryover) body.

Top: Family favorite - the 1961 Rambler Classic station wagon. Bottom: Still handsome despite six years in production, the 1961 Rambler Classic four-door sedan.

65

Top: For 1961, Anderson and Teague came up with this "Euro" look front end redesign. Bottom: 1961 Ambassador station wagon.

Ambassador sales had never been very high, about 24,000 in each of the preceding years, so perhaps it was felt that more radical styling would help. At the sales rate it was running, it certainly couldn't hurt it much.

It didn't, but Anderson's radical front didn't help sales at all; they fell to about 18,000 Ambassadors for 1961. The less expensive car did better. The new American, its styling criticized by some, sold very well ... over 135,000 units, a new record for the American.

But 1961 was another recession year for business, and sales from the fall through the winter were off substantially. A spring upswing, driven by a hefty and expensive marketing push by AMC, got sales going again, but not enough to offset the slow first half. Worldwide wholesale shipments were 392,971 of which 8,142 were the Metropolitan. This was a drop from 1960, but the entire industry was off even more. In August 1961, Rambler became the third best-selling car in America, displacing Plymouth.

Also in 1961, an agreement was signed with Industrias Kaiser Argentina, the South American subsidiary of Kaiser Motors, to allow for assembly of Ramblers by IKA for the Latin American market. This seemingly insignificant move would foreshadow later agreements between Kaiser Jeep and AMC, as well as between AMC and the company that would soon become owner of IKA, Renault. The postwar Kaiser was still being produced and sold by IKA, but its days were numbered, and IKA was looking for a more modern car to produce. The Rambler seemed like a good bet, and AMC was interested, as an earlier study had decided that AMC's best hope for international expansion lay in

Rear three-quarter view of the 1961 American shows subtle sculpture and "eyebrow" theme.

67

Although they look cute today, in 1961 the Metropolitan looked out of date. Production ended in mid-1960, with in-stock vehicles sold through 1961 and 1962.

the Latin American market. AMC was about to start on a South American expansion that would help it become one of the largest exporters of American cars in the seventies. Added to the news of capturing third place in America, it seemed to bode well for the future.

Third place or no, it was still an off year for AMC as sales dropped below the billion dollar mark, to $875,723,798, a result of the lower auto sales as well as lower sales of Kelvinator appliances. It seems that no one noticed that a part of the drop was also a result of a poorer model mix, that is, a higher percentage of lower-priced Americans being sold than ever before. Nowhere in the annual reports is that mentioned, although it's possible that the situation was considered to be a temporary aberration caused by the recession.

Net profits dropped to $23,578,894, and the employee count dropped to 28,641. Working capital went up to a very healthy $103 million, an increase of $7 million, so the company was not in any trouble yet. It just meant that a closer watch on costs had to be maintained. There was some concern entering the 1962 model year because there wouldn't be any really new car for 1962, and imports of the Metropolitan had been halted in 1960. That decision was made as the company continued to put its resources behind the Rambler nameplate. With the expansion of Kenosha's production capacity and with all-new Ramblers coming onstream in 1963 and 1964, the Metropolitan was being left behind. It couldn't be built in America at anywhere near the low cost needed, and the cost of retooling the English plant seemed inadvisable at a time when the Kenosha plant had already been expanded. Romney felt that the better cost position of the American would allow him to sell the

American for not much more than the Metropolitan, and the American, he felt, was a much better value. He was right, but he was forgetting that some people, more and more each day, were deciding to buy smaller cars because they saw smallness itself as a virtue. American Motors had brought out the original Rambler in 1950 based on that very argument, that smallness itself was appealing. Either AMC had forgotten that by 1961, or it had decided that the 100-inch wheelbase was as small as small should be. It was too bad, for dropping the Met meant that AMC had no four-cylinder car to compete with the imports on fuel economy, not a big point in 1961, but it would be later. The project that had started to design a new Met ended before it really got going; the design never got beyond pencil sketches.

Roy Chapin, as the head of the international division, had the job of telling the Austin people that American Motors was ending the Metropolitan program. "It had been decided," Chapin said, "to end the Metropolitan and concentrate on the American, as that way we could earn a manufacturing profit

Three views of the 1962 Rambler American four-door. Note the revised grille.

1962 Metropolitan hardtop.

as well as a sales profit, which would be more than the distributor profit we were making on the Met." There were plenty of leftover Metropolitans in stock, and AMC rebadged them as 1962s before they were shipped to dealers.

For 1962 there were some refinements to the Rambler lineup. The biggest change was in the Ambassador. Stung by the poor sales of the restyled 1961 Ambassador and unwilling to spend money to face-lift a car that was in the final year of a long model run, American Motors discontinued the 117-inch wheelbase and built the 1962 Ambassador on the same 108-inch wheelbase as the Rambler Classic. The public hardly noticed, for the two series had shared bodies for years anyway, and the elongated front end of the Ambassador had gone unnoticed by many. The radical face-lift of the 1961 Ambassador was junked as the 1962 used the same basic grille as the Classic. It was decided that a V-8 Classic and a V-8 Ambassador would be redundant as long as they shared the same chassis, so for 1962 the Classic was offered only as a six and became, once again, the Rambler Classic 6. The 195.6 cid engine, back for another year, was again offered in cast iron or aluminum blocks.

For 1962, the most expensive American Motors car was the Rambler Ambassador as the old "Ambassador by Rambler" nomenclature was dropped with the larger wheelbase. It was all evidence of the consolidation of the line into a completely integrated range of cars bearing the successful Rambler nameplate.

The Classic series received one new body style, a two-door sedan, that dealers had been requesting for years. The Ambassador series did get revised rear styling and different taillights to be a bit fancier than the Classics and also offered a two-door sedan.

Romney was back in the sales brochures in 1962, this time emphasizing quality and safety. He had a big advantage in the safety department, as American Motors equipped all Ramblers with a twin circuit master cylinder, something only Cadillac and Rolls-Royce had at that time.

The 1962 Ramblers held on to third place in industry sales despite carryover styling and despite an improved market. By the end of the fiscal year, 478,132 units had been sold worldwide, 434,486 in the United States and 43,646 elsewhere. It was a strong showing for the United States and a dramatic improvement in foreign sales, a result of the new Canadian operation and the move into

Three views of the 1962 Ambassador. This was the first Ambassador to wear the Rambler name, and it used the 108-inch wheelbase. Note the unique rear end treatment.

71

Top: The 125 hp 195.6 cid six-cylinder engine. Bottom: The double safety brake system with tandem master cylinder was standard on all Ramblers for 1962.

1962 Rambler Classic station wagon.

Argentina, Switzerland and Australia. Profits improved to $34,240,621 on sales of $1,056,395,059 as AMC went over the billion dollar mark in sales for just the second time in its history. It looked as if things were back to normal.

One important change occurred in December 1961 as sales of the 1962 Rambler were taking off again and tooling for the all-new 1963 Rambler was being ordered. Ed Anderson, very happy with the success of the 1961 American, a job he called "the best face-lift of an existing design I have ever done," and very excited about his all-new 1963 Ramblers, went to his superiors and requested a promotion to vice president of styling. He felt he deserved the job and he was right. Despite a few miscalculations, such as the 1961 Ambassador, Ed had fielded a series of new cars that had catapulted Rambler from the back of the bunch to third place in industry sales, while the other independent automakers were falling apart. Anderson had all the responsibility of a vice president, and now he wanted the title and the prestige that went with it.

He should have been awarded the position, but Anderson's career at AMC had started on the wrong foot when George Mason had chosen him instead of the son of an AMC vice president who had also wanted the job. He had disagreements with the engineering department that had festered over the years. When he asked to be promoted to vice president, he was told that if he was unhappy with his position at AMC he should resign. Stunned and angry, Anderson tendered his resignation effective December 1961. He had been the only head of design AMC ever had and now he was going. He stayed around Detroit for a while, had in-depth discussions at Chrysler about becoming their vice president of styling, but in the end decided to pack in cold Detroit and head south. He retired to Mexico.

73

Then the other shoe dropped. Romney asked for a leave of absence to explore the possibility of making a run for the governorship of Michigan, effective Feb. 12, 1962. The board, of course, had to either grant his request or risk having him just quit, so an unpaid leave of absence was granted. But after looking at his options, Romney decided to exit the automobile world and enter the world of politics. On Nov. 15, 1962, the board of directors accepted Romney's resignation.

Roy Abernethy, vice president of sales, was immediately elevated to president and chief executive officer. Richard Cross, who had been vice chairman in Romney's absence, received the title of chairman. It is important to note that AMC, for the first time, now had a separate chairman and president.

Richard Cross (left), chairman of the board, and Roy Abernethy, president of AMC.

American Motors also had a new director of styling, that archaic term that AMC used to describe the duties that a vice president of styling did at other companies. Richard Teague was fairly new to the company, hired in 1958 by Ed Anderson, but he had good credentials. Teague was a graduate of California's Art Center School in Los Angeles, considered then and today to be the top school for transportation design. Teague had also taken a work study course in auto design at General Motors. He had been assigned to an Oldsmobile experimental styling studio, a place called Plant 8. In a show of wit for which he would later become well-known, Teague always referred to that hated spot as "Planet 8." After a brief stint there he bounced around, finally landing in Packard, where he became head of Packard styling. This was a prestige job, for although Packard was slowly losing volume and sales to the more aggressive Cadillac, the company was still held in awe by most of the world, and rightly so. Packard cars, the saying went, were "built by gentlemen and sold to gentlemen by gentlemen."

What Teague and the rest of the industry soon realized was that Packard's days were numbered and not with high numbers, either. After spurning the advances of George Mason in 1946, Packard had wasted time and made a few bad decisions until finally, in 1954, the company made its worst decision when it bought out the ailing Studebaker Corporation. Dick Teague was destined to be the last head of Packard styling in Detroit, and by 1958 was in need of a job.

Anderson had taken him on, evidently realizing the talent that the designer had, and now Richard

Designer Richard Teague (center) early in his long career at AMC.

Teague had his old boss' job. There was no need to break in the new chief as he had been working on the 1961, 1962 and 1963 projects alongside Anderson and knew the program well. Advance work had already begun on the all-new Rambler American for 1964, including full-size clay models.

By the end of 1962, as the all-new 1963 Ramblers were just reaching the new car showrooms of a dealer body that had not had an all-new car since 1956, American Motors was being led by a new chairman of the board, a new president, and had a new head of styling. It was an awful lot of change for such a conservative company, but the problem was not that the company was conservative. The problem was that American Motors had always been run by a single man, dictatorial style. That single man had so far been exactly the right man for the job. Mason had been a visionary, able to foresee a problem before others could think of it and able to conceive a solution before it was too late. Romney had been the faith healer, able to hold the company together and get all the elements of it working together towards a common goal in the face of ridicule and opposition. Mason had known the future would be tough, and had groomed a successor that he knew would be able to lead the troops in the right direction. But had the board of directors chosen the right man to succeed Romney? Roy Chapin remembers that the board felt that what was needed most to head the company was a sales-oriented person. In the fall of 1962, the new Ramblers, products of a very expensive tooling program, were unveiled to the public. And what cars they were!

When the decision had been made in 1960 to develop an all-new line of Ramblers, it was a given that the design would have to last for several years on the market, the same as the 1956 Rambler had done, with only minor face-lifting and perhaps a reskinning in later years. The reason now was the same as the reason back then, to save on the cost of tooling. In 1956, that had been critical because AMC was too poor to retool more than the one car, and could not, at the volume it sold at first, have been able to afford a major change every year or two, the way Ford and GM did. It was now important to save on retooling costs in order to keep overhead low enough to be able to price the Rambler lower than the competition, while still providing for an adequate profit margin, a hard trick to do in

This clay mock-up of the 1963 Ambassador still wears the Nash-style squeeze door handles and odd wheel opening for rear wheels. It was probably made in 1960.

This mock-up, with aluminum foil-covered clay bumper, was picked as the production design for the 1963 Ambassador. Note the 1961 American in the background.

the auto industry, as Studebaker was finding out. Simply refusing to restyle the car wouldn't work, as the public still preferred buying a new car that looked new. It was a tightrope walk for AMC, this business of retaining the basic style of a car while redesigning enough of it to appeal to new car buyers, while maintaining a low price and a decent profit margin, but the old team had done it and done it well. And the old team was the one that had designed the 1963 cars.

Good old Ed Anderson was excited by the project. He mocked up some full-size clay models of the design direction he felt the company should take, and the change was startling. What was shown were prototypes of an envelope-bodied sedan with an almost European profile, a look of understated elegance at a Rambler price. The protoypes were designed on a wheelbase of 112 inches, four inches longer than the 1962 Ramblers Classics, to retain good legroom while allowing for the lowered roofline that Anderson knew would be the style of the sixties. In keeping with the Rambler tradition, Anderson's team kept the front end overhang tight, but allowed a somewhat longer and much lower rear overhang. Rooflines were squared, an effort that had begun with the 1961 American and one that Anderson felt so strongly about that he had argued with his boss and with Romney himself. In a move that separated the 1963 Rambler from the rest of the cars in the lower cost end of the market, the 1963 had the first curved glass side windows used in a popular-priced car. This was the focus of another argument that the designer had with the engineering department. The engineering people felt that the extra cost of the curved glass windows was a waste, money that could be better spent developing a new engine or used to increase productivity. The cost accountants, used as they were to searching out ways to save pennies in manufacturing costs, were appalled at the thought of adding expense to the product. Romney was in on the discussions, and many meetings were held over the issue of whether or not to use the curved glass side windows. The cost was high, at least in the way auto costs are figured. Engineering said it would add $2 to the cost of building each car. Romney wasn't worried about $2, but he was very distressed about $2 times the expected 400,000 Ramblers, a total of $800,000 that would come directly out of the bottom line.

In an emotional meeting, Anderson explained his belief that the Big Three would soon be using curved glass side windows in all their cars, and, as the 1963 Rambler's body would be the basis for the 1964 through 1969 Ramblers, if curved glass was not incorporated in the design at the onset, then the Rambler would soon look old and stale next to the competition. That convinced Romney, which, of course, settled the question.

The all-new cars also featured a new design for the door openings, called Uni-side, and it was a great improvement in car building. The fifty or so small pieces that were ordinarily welded together to make the side door openings were replaced by two larger stampings, an inner and an outer, that allowed for much tighter clearances in door fits and eliminated dust and water leaks while maintaining a rattlefree fit.

Coil spring suspension was used all the way around, and the wheel size was reduced to 14 inches for a lower look. That old steady, the 195.6 cid cast six-cylinder motor, was back again and again in cast iron or aluminum block. The interior of the car was light and airy, always a trademark of Anderson work, as he felt that larger windows greatly reduced the claustrophobic tendencies of compact cars. A switch was made in the door handles to a more conventional push button type, even though it was more costly. Some prospective buyers had disliked the squeeze-type door handles that began as a Nash feature and were continued, by Anderson, on the Ramblers. Anderson felt strongly that the squeeze-type handles were an important styling feature, but he lost that argument.

Perhaps the most striking feature of the 1963 Rambler was the cleanness of the basic design. The

Top: All new for 1963 was this Rambler Ambassador sedan. Bottom: Handsome styling marked the 1963 Rambler Ambassador station wagon.

SPECIAL AWARD ISSUE

MOTOR TREND

FEBRUARY 1963 · 50c
60c IN CANADA

1963
CAR of the YEAR

RAMBLER

*In February 1963, **Motor Trend** magazine named the entire lineup of Ramblers the "1963 Car of the Year."*

slab sides, large windows, and neat overhangs all hinted at Mercedes styling without being a blatant copy. And unlike the European cars of the time, the Rambler did have body sculpturing, but it was subtle enough to not be a focal point, only an enhancement. The rear quarter panels in particular

One-Year Wonder. The Rambler American hardtop was new for 1963 and built that one year only.

Early clay mock-up, by Ed Anderson and Dick Teague, of the proposed new American for 1963-'64.

showed the highlighting and smooth scalloping of which Anderson was proud. The trim was refined, more elegant than before and more functional, as the side mouldings now served as ding protection as well. The grille was then and still is now a point of controversy. An inverted V in profile, Anderson felt it provided instant identification, which it did, as the Rambler looked like no other car on the road. Some people in the company thought it was an odd look.

The public must have liked the grille, and the rest of the styling for that matter, because the 1963 Rambler sold like hotcakes. The company decided to continue the practice of building the Classic and Ambassador on the same wheelbase, both labeled as Ramblers, with the Classic offered in six-cylinder models while the Ambassadors would be eight-cylinder cars. The brochures bragged about offering 13 solid colors and a whopping 43 two-tone combinations, as well as a choice of three-speed transmission, three-speed with overdrive, and fully automatic or E-stick semi-automatic transmissions.

The dealer body set a new record, as wholesale orders for Ramblers hit 511,048. The cost of tooling for the new car was a major drag on earnings, but still, profits hit $37,807,205, a highly acceptable number considering the expenditures involved. Sales were helped along by the American, which contributed about 95,000 units to the total, despite being in the third year of production without a restyling. The American line had received a new model, a pert two-door hardtop Anderson's

This mock-up for a new American had two different grille themes.

This completed clay mock-up was Anderson's proposal for the new American for 1964.

82

studio had put together to jazz up the line. But the excitement had all been in the Classic/Ambassador series. The public loved it, while dealers called it a selling machine. The company called it a record-setter, and Motor Trend magazine, in its February 1963 issue, called it the "Car of the Year."

That was the first time American Motors had ever earned that award, but with Dick Teague working on a new Rambler American for 1964, it looked as if the 1963 award was just the start of something big. In January 1963, when Roy Abernethy pushed through a change in the lineup that added a V-8 engine to the option list of the Classic, it seemed as if a new direction was being considered, perhaps to change the image of the Rambler from a value car to a sexy car. It was too early to say, it was embryonic, and it was mostly in the mind of Roy Abernethy. It never occurred to most people that the successor to Romney might not want to move in the same direction his boss had moved. Those people, and the stockholders of American Motors, would soon learn a lot about Roy Abernethy, most of it much too late.

Very clean, simple design for proposed new American.

Rear three-quarter view of Anderson's proposal for the American. Note the Chevy II in the background. This photo was taken in the AMC design studios.

This rare photograph, never before shown to the public, shows the small two-door sedan called Apache, a version of the American line being worked on.

This clay mock-up, probably done in 1960 or 1961, shows lines that are becoming more like the actual 1964 American. Note the body indentation at the door bottoms that matches the 1963 Rambler Classic.

This unique rear photo shows two completely different designs on one body. Neither one was used.

NEW RAMBLER CLASSIC V-8

"... has tremendous appeal
for buyers looking for quality
transportation and operating
economy at a price. For value and
for good basic transportation it
would be hard to find a better buy"

Now read what else Tom McCahill says
about the '63 Rambler Classic V-8 ⟶

The addition of V-8 models in the Classic line in mid-1963 was perhaps the first sign of the coming change in direction for the company.

Chapter 3

1964-1969
The End of the Road for Rambler

When the books finally closed on the 1963 model year, Roy Abernethy could look with pride on his first year as the new head of American Motors. Wholesale unit sales of Ramblers reached a new high, over 511,000 cars, and profits were certainly good. The working capital balance was $118,867,772, the highest it had ever been. The entire lineup of new Ramblers had won Motor Trend's "Car of the Year" award, and the stockholders, dealers and employees were all satisfied with management. Abernethy could point to all those positives and merge them with the plans he and his staff had made for 1964 to form a veritable collage of good news.

The problem was that most of the successes of 1963 were the result of the management that had just departed, namely George Romney and the skillfull work of designer Ed Anderson.

Abernethy's most noteworthy influence on the 1963 program was his decision, as soon as Romney was gone, to revise the product plan decided on in 1961 of marketing the Classic as a six-cylinder car and the Ambassador as a V-8 car. AMC offered a V-8 engine as an option on the Classic beginning in January 1963. One retired AMC executive recalled that decision years later and the effect it had on him. "This," the executive said, "I count as the beginning of American Motors' downturn." Abernethy also disliked the image American Motors had in the market, which was as a safe, sensible product, high in quality and value but more of a mature person's car. One executive recalled, "I asked Romney if he wasn't concerned that so many of our cars were seen driven in the slow lane on the highway." "No," Romney replied, "just so long as there are a lot of them."

Romney understood that to try to compete in the annual restyling game was a sucker's bet that could only be lost. A small company like AMC would quickly go broke trying to match tooling dollars with the Big Three. A more conservative style was needed, one that, while perhaps not the last word in fashion, would stay in style longer so that its selling life could be extended. This conserva-

The 1964 Ambassador featured a new grille and new hardtop models.

tive approach would save the company millions of dollars in tooling costs, which in turn would ensure that the smallest competitor would always be profitable and would always be around. It all boiled down to the cost of tooling amortization, and Romney's plans would always keep that vital fact in the forefront. Quality, reliability and value would be the primary selling points of AMC cars, and Romney felt there were enough buyers out there who appreciated quality and value to make the Rambler a lasting success.

Top: Rambler Classic 770 for 1964. Bottom: New hardtop styling was now available for Classic and Ambassaor.

The Rambler was a bit of a prig designwise, but that, after all, was the market AMC was after. In the fifties, Romney had to change Mason's original goal of combining companies to create a Big Four automaker, and had to adopt a "hit 'em where they ain't" strategy to survive. The decision to sink or swim with the Rambler had been the right decison, and to Romney's credit, he had figured out that riddle in time to save the company. How close he came to failure could be seen in Indiana, where the Studebaker company had reached the same conclusion in 1958, and rushed the 1959 Lark into production. Studebaker, of course, had seen how well Rambler had done in 1957 and 1958, so it was easier to make up their minds by the time they finally did.

But changing course in 1959 was too late for Studebaker. Although they revived for a time, they never really got healthy again and had to leave the car business in the sixties. In comparison, the Rambler was selling in strong numbers in 1960-1962, and hit a new record for 1963, all because of its carefully nutured image and the inherent excellence of the cars. Another competitor was likewise nurturing its hard-won reputation for quality and reliabilty. Volkswagen of America had seen its sales in the United States climb from two cars in 1949 to the point where it now was the best-selling import in America, outpacing the upstart Renault.

Abernethy, however, was convinced that AMC's image as a conservative family car would turn around someday soon and bite it on the hand. He did have some reason to worry, for at Ford a new car had come out in April 1964 as a 1965 model, and it was selling out to the bare walls. The 1965 Mustang became the most talked about new car since the advent of the Ford Model A in 1928. There were other signs before then, though, that the market might be moving more upscale.

In 1963, Ford had introduced a new car, called the Fairlane, which was smaller than the full-sized Ford but larger than the Falcon. This meant, of course, that the Fairlane competed head-to-head with the Rambler Classic. The Fairlane sold so well that in 1964 Chevy moved into the new segment, so-called "senior compact," with the Chevy Chevelle. Oldsmobile, Buick and Pontiac all had midsized cars and compacts, too, as the American car market splintered into several size categories at once. Pontiac introduced a new sub-segment when it dropped a huge V-8 engine into the intermediate-sized Tempest to create the GTO. Against all this new and frightening competition, Abernethy had only the tried and true Ramblers, and he felt they wouldn't be enough. In fairness, it should be noted that the competition was much heavier in the Rambler's segment of the market than it ever had been before, and it looked to get heavier before it got lighter. With some valid concerns and some worries about the future, Abernethy entered the auto market for the 1964 model year.

The 1964 lineup of new Ramblers was the strongest it had ever been. The Rambler Classics of 1956-1961 had all been four-door cars, either sedans, hardtops or station wagons. Even the 1962 lineup had just one plain two-door model to break up the string of four-doors that were offered to the public. 1963's redesign had allowed Anderson to tool for a volume-built two-door sedan to go along with the four-door sedans and stationwagons. For 1964 the Classic line was further enhanced with a new and very attractive two-door hardtop model offered in the top-of-the-line 770 series trim. The Ambassador also received the hardtop body. However, for 1964 the Ambassadors were offered only in top-line 990 trim as the lower-priced 880 Ambassadors were dropped to make way for the V-8 Classic series.

Dick Teague redesigned a few items on the Classic/Ambassadors, perhaps to make them more reflective of his own taste or perhaps just because the sales department wanted something new. Whatever the reason, it was a neat job. Teague fashioned a new grille to replace the "electric shaver" look of the 1963 cars, a really handsome and cost effective bit of work that still featured the quad

90

headlamps that were a Rambler styling trademark. The front end appearance was certainly improved by this move. Side trim was made more bold and was used more liberally on all the series, the better to impart a quality appearance. Interiors became more luxurious, and exterior colors more muted.

Top: 1964 Ambassador hardtop. Bottom: 1964 Rambler Classic station wagon.

But the big news for 1964 had nothing to do with the Classic/Ambassadors. For 1964, Teague created a completely redesigned and reengineered Rambler American on an all-new chassis. This new American was the culmination of the consolidated chassis project that was envisioned in 1959. That program consisted of an all-new American based on the Classic series but shortened and narrowed to cut material costs while sharing enough basic tooling to secure a substantial savings.

A sharp eye can see the identical body indentation just above the rocker panels, necessitated by the sharing of doors on the two-door Classics and Americans. Underbody panels were shared between the two series as well.

Externally, the new American was more different than similar, and it was a beauty, one of the best-looking economy sedans of the sixties. Some designers say it was the best. The new American rode a wheelbase of 106 inches, six more than in the old series, but overall length grew just four inches, evidence of Teague's commitment to the idea of compact dimensions and tight overhangs. It was lower and wider than previous Americans. The increase in wheelbase had allowed for the rear seat to be moved forward of the rear wheel wells, increasing rear seat width by a whopping 12 inches and allowing for full six-passenger seating instead of the "tight for five" of the old American. Because he was doing a full redesign instead of a reskin or face-lift, Teague was able to lower the beltline of the car to improve appearance and to substantially improve the car's side profile.

Because this new American was going to cost the company a ton of money to retool, it was going to have to sell in even larger numbers than the 1961-1963 face-lifted cars had. To make sure it would, it was decided to increase the range of body styles in the line to increase sales and to ensure that this vital market segment would be a major profit center for the company. American Motors had to get a larger share of the low-price compact car market if it was to reach its profit goals. Accordingly, the 1964 American series included, in the lowest price 220 trim, a two-door sedan, four-door sedan, and four-door station wagon. The 330 series echoed this range of body types in slightly fan-

This American prototype shows roofline similar to the 1963 Classic; note the interesting side window treatment.

92

The styling of this station wagon clay mock-up is similar to the actual 1964 American.

Another view of the American prototype.

93

This American appears smaller than the production 1964 car.

With the exception of the two chrome strips running along the body sides, this clay is very similar to the production American for 1964.

Top: The first all-new American since 1950 was the 1964 American. Bottom: The handsome sedan sold well.

cier trim. The new top-of-the-line 440 series, however, consisted of a sharp two-door hardtop, in five- or six-passenger versions, a well-trimmed four-door sedan, and an exceptionally pretty convertible.

Teague introduced, although it wasn't mentioned at the time, two of his more noticeable trademarks, the tunneled headlight and the horizontal bar grille. It was rumored that the rounded headlight shape was pirated from the Chrysler Turbine dream car, and that might be true, but later redesigns tend to go against that idea. At any rate, it was a first class design by AMC's new head stylist, and the public went for it in a big way. The new American was an unqualified sales success and deservedly so.

Change had been coming to American Motors, but it had come in small increments, slowly, year by year. 1963 was the first year that all cars sold at American Motors dealers were Ramblers; the Ambassador by Rambler nameplate was changed to Rambler Ambassador in early 1962, while the last handful of rebadged leftover Metropolitans were finally sold out at the end of 1962. The 1964 was the most comprehensive lineup of body styles in AMC history, two-doors, four-doors, hardtops, sedans, station wagons and convertibles. It was right to continue to change, for to stand still in the auto business is to allow oneself to get run over.

The trick was to enact changes that would add to the perceived value of the car, and in so doing, to the image of the company as well. It was not enough to be able to pay large dividends to the stock-

95

holders without winning the praise of the daily newspaper and the all-important auto press, for if an inadequate image was projected to the press, it would be instantly reflected back to the public and in even worse light in the next day's newspaper or magazine. It is important to remember that an image is a hard won thing. The Nash and Hudson nameplates were discontinued and were looked down on as losers. Through the determined efforts of George Romney, that loser image had not transferred to the Rambler. Indeed, the Rambler in 1964 had a public persona that many companies would have preferred for their own.

American Motors and Roy Abernethy learned a hard lesson in the auto business in December 1963. The Studebaker Corporation, which had attempted to compete head-to-head with the Big Three until it had been run almost into the ground, had switched to building compact cars in 1959 after seeing how well Rambler was doing. But entering the compact car market in 1959, instead of 1956 as Rambler had done (or even 1950 with the original Nash Rambler), had not allowed Studebaker enough time to build a reputation as a quality compact car builder. When the Big Three began to enter the compact market in 1960-1961, the Studebaker dealer body deserted in droves, canceling sales agreements that had been signed in 1959 and picking up new franchises with the Big Three. AMC, by virtue of its longevity in the market, held onto its dealers and had prospered. Studebaker tried to hold together throughout 1961-1963 while it tried to formulate a strategy for the future. For a while, it had planned a shared lineup similar to Rambler's, where an all-new Lark would share components with a new, smaller Studebaker. But its thinner resources ran out sooner. In the fall of 1963, its hopes were pinned to a heavily face-lifted Lark. By December 1963, it was apparent to all that the new Lark was a failure. The main Studebaker plant in South Bend, Indiana, one of the oldest in the industry, was closed for good as Studebaker's small needs could be adequately met by its tiny Canadian factory. Although technically still in the business, Studebaker was never a factor in automobiles again.

American Motors had escaped the fate of so many independent automakers. Through its program to consolidate to one brand name and one unifying theme, it had carved out a niche for itself, a profitable one at that. And its third-place finish had shown to the world that it had moxie and staying power. It was on course with a new model program that had, in just two years, completely revamped and modernized the entire lineup of Ramblers.

Yet, for all the money sunk into new models and new body styles, for all the cash put into new plant equipment and tooling, when the 1964 model year ended, sales had actually dropped. It was not a dramatic drop nor a frightening drop. Dollar volume was $1,009,470,701 against 1963's $1,132,356,298. It was the fourth time in AMC history sales had topped the billion dollar mark. And profits were fair though down to $26,226,735 from 1963's $37,807,205. More worrisome details were a bit deeper in the annual report. The $11.5 million drop in net income had come from a drop of nearly $33 million dollars in gross (pre-tax) profits. Despite the sharp drop in profits, cash dividends were actually higher, $21.8 million versus $18.7 million in 1963. Even more ominous, net working capital had dropped to $94,653,625, the lowest since 1958. A steadily increasing working capital account had been one of the hallmarks of George Romney, reflecting a fiscal conservatism he had learned at Nash. Nash was a well-run company and, after all, it had been the one with the cash when the merger of Hudson and Nash came about. Romney's fiscal conservatism had stood the stockholders good stead when times were hard in the mid-1950s.

Now Abernethy seemed to play a bit looser and faster with money. One of the reasons for the decrease in dollar sales volume and the decrease in profits, according to Abernethy, was "a lower proportion of sales in higher-priced models." Another reason given was "increased tooling amortization." History may fault Abernethy for the increased tooling costs in 1964, as that reflected a certain disregard for costs, but these charges were for the 1965 models that were planned to sell in large volumes. Yet it's interesting to note his mention of a poorer mix of models, i.e. too many low-priced cars and not enough higher-priced cars. Even though Romney had always insisted on a full range of models to broaden his market reach, he had never used sales of too many lower-priced models as an excuse for lower profits. Wages, salaries, and benefit costs were all lower for 1964, reflecting the lower unit volume of 455,073 cars, so some analysts could point to that as a sign of fiscal responsibility, as it was. The value of stockholders' equity also looked good, an all-time high of $278,718,229.

The new American had scored a big hit; over 163,000 were built -- a production record for that model. The V-8 Classic was a minor contender at just under 60,000 units built. While sales of the V-8 Classic were up, sales of the six-cylinder were down badly. A special model of the Classic was built in limited numbers to showcase an all-new six-cylinder engine that was just going into production, an engine that would be the mainstay of the line for the next 20 years, the 232 cubic inch Torque Command Six. The special car developed to show off this new engine was a Classic two-door hardtop painted in solar yellow with a black painted roof and black vinyl bucket seat interior. Called the Typhoon, just 2,520 of these handsome hardtops were made and offered only in the 1964 model year.

The sales drop was not of fatal proportions. American Motors had seen sales drop before, in 1961 -- coincidentally another year when a new American had been introduced. While the competition was getting stronger, especially in the senior compact segment, which would soon be renamed the intermediate segment, American Motors had been selling against similarly sized cars since the 1959

Rare and pretty: The Typhoon showcased the new 232 cid six-cylinder engine.

Studebaker Lark. AMC only had the market for cars below standard size all to itself in 1956 through 1958, when it had been a weak company, and this was not the same company it had been in 1956. Debt had been completely paid off during the Romney years. Working capital had been added every year to build and maintain a strong cash position, both to provide a fund for rainy day emergencies and to save the expense of borrowing from banks to fund growth.

The plan for the future was for American Motors to be a more focused company, working with a well-developed plan. The product line now consisted entirely of Ramblers, one brand name for the three series of automobiles. The American series was the low-priced small or compact car. The Classic was the mid-sized "family car." And the Ambassador was the up-market luxury product, compact in exterior size but loaded with trim and features to appeal to a higher income market and offered only as an eight-cylinder vehicle.

The most important element of this product range was that they all shared the same basic body/chassis. That was the whole reason for going with the expensive product program of 1963-1964 in the first place. Romney had seen, just as in the fifties, that AMC would not be able to compete model for model with the Big Three if it tried to restyle its products every two or three years the way that Ford, Chevy, and Chrysler could (and would) do. The cost of such tooling would bankrupt AMC. What Romney had envisioned, and Ed Anderson put into metal, was a three model range, sharing body tooling in such a way as to allow substantial cost savings. These cost savings would then be passed along to the customer by allowing for a lower price on the Rambler American, and for more standard features on the Classics and Ambassadors to make them all better values. Romney believed that he could win in the market, in the segments he carefully chose, if he could offer better value.

In an interview in *Collectible Automobile*, April 1989, George Romney had this to say in explanation: "Actually, the strongest of all Rambler lines was the one that was introduced just as I was leaving the company -- the 1963 model. And the strongest part of that series was the (new) American, which wasn't scheduled to come out until the next year. But before it was introduced, why they'd scrambled the whole concept of a simplified line, with three models -- Ambassador, Classic and American -- sharing essentially the same stampings. The idea was that we could focus the advantage of volume on the pricing of the American. We could have priced it down very close to the Volkswagen Beetle, and of course it was much more of a car. But that never happened, you see. My successor, who started out with Packard, reverted to the Big Three philosophy and scrambled the whole picture. He spent $200 million in the first two years after he took over, trying to make the Rambler more of a big car. And they went steadily downhill."

Of the 1963 Rambler Classic/Ambassador, and the plans he had made to market it, he said, "If you'll take a look at it, you'll see that the styling was really very simple. The concept was that *style was no longer a major factor* with people who were basically interested in a good, dependable piece of transportation -- one that still looked good, along the lines of a Mercedes-Benz." (The emphasis has been put in by the author to highlight what went wrong with AMC, at least in the 1964-1969 period.)

What happened is that Roy Abernethy changed a line of cars that was designed to appeal to an untraditional consumer/car buyer. Enlarging on his strategy of "hitting 'em where they ain't," Romney hoped to win sales by offering better value to the customer. It had saved the company in 1956 when the Rambler had sold well, even though its price was higher than Ford and Chevy, to buyers interested in value for the dollar. It had served as the spiritual foundation of American Motors even through the success years of the early sixties when face-lifted 1960,1961 and 1962 Ramblers sold well, again on the basis of value. When the cost advantage of the new, unified line together with the all-new styling and new models were considered fully, it was a sound and correct plan for competing with the giants of the marketplace. George Romney, in a 1992 interview, further stated that the styling "was supposed to last for several years, with only minor changes," again to cut costs. Romney knew that by refusing to follow the annual restyling race with the Big Three, he could control his costs to a point where he could offer the consumer a better value, thus generating good sales while still making the profit margin he needed to make. This was the entire plan for the Rambler line. It was a well laid plan, one that was proven to be historically correct. By staying within the guideline fundamentals of low tooling costs and styling continuity, the plan would provide American Motors with continued success.

The problem was that Abernethy didn't believe it, and he was the man who now ran the company. He still had to report to a board of directors, but he held a big advantage there. After all, Abernethy was in sales all his life, and even his detractors had to admit that he was a salesman par excellence. Romney and Mason had brought him into American Motors to rebuild its dealer organization, and the gregarious Abernethy had performed splendidly. No, he had no problem getting corporate approval for any program he liked. He could sell the idea to the board the same way he could sell a truckload of Ramblers to a dealer.

He was determined to change the Rambler image. As one public relations executive recalled, "Two days after Roy Abernethy was officially made president, I had to go in the board room and arrange for a tape he was going to make for some radio show. And he said to me, 'You've got to help me get rid of this Romney image.'"

Adding the V-8 engine to the Classic in mid-1963 seemed to increase sales, albeit not by much. And an optimist could point out that sales of the V-8 Classic had increased in 1964 while the six-cylinder car had suffered a big decrease. The only reason the V-8 Classics sold better in 1964 was because they were on the market for 12 full months versus only eight months in 1963. Being a new product and the boss' favorite, the V-8 cars received additional advertising push. But the die was struck, and the company began, slowly at first, to make a sea change. The 1964 brochures emphasized the top-of-the-line models in each series as well as the glamourous new hardtop body styles, all reasonable approaches. But it allowed very little space for showing off the Classic station wagons, which, although not glamour stars, were traditionally top-selling models.

In the annual report for 1964, Abernethy noted that $42 million was spent on tooling for the new 232 cid six-cylinder engine, and that the three millionth Rambler was produced during the year. But he went on to note, "To some extent buyers continue to identify Rambler primarily with conservative design and economy in a period of increased customer interest in extra options, luxury features and higher performance. Rambler has been moving with this trend, and the lag in identity should be amply corrected by the 1965 Rambler models, which represent the most sweeping changes in our history." This showed Abernethy's lack of commitment to the original product program, and it also showed an amazing amount of naivete if he felt that Rambler's hard-won reputation could be changed in one more model year. Still, Roy Abernethy was determined to make the Rambler into a new image, a new contender in the perennial sales battle. Abernethy now planned to spend whatever it took to change the lineup to more closely correspond with what the Big Three offered. He began to take on GM, Ford, and Chrysler head-to-head in their territory. And, as he said, 1965 would be the year.

For 1965, Abernethy made good on his promise. The 1965 Rambler American was mostly a carryover; it had been all new for 1964 and had sold like nickel cigars. The new 232 cid engine was now available as an option on the American, while the old flathead version of the 195.6 cid engine was standard equipment. Sporty floor shifters for the standard or automatic transmission were now available, too, as were wire wheel covers, all evidence of Abernethy's new approach.

There were bigger changes for the Classic, billed, appropriately enough, as the all-new Rambler Classic, the biggest, most powerful Classics ever built. A sharp convertible was added to the lineup, a welcome addition for it was a real beauty. It was just unfortunate that the market for convertibles had peaked and was heading into a downturn. The volume models -- the sedans and station wagons -- were new, too. Not all new, regardless of what the ads said, but new enough. Dick Teague, using

Despite pleasing lines, American sales fell in 1965.

100

For 1965, the Rambler line-up consisted of three distinct series. Top: American. Center: Classic. Bottom: Ambassador. All three were available in hardtop models, as shown.

101

A different face -- the 1965 Ambassador.

the same 112-inch wheelbase as the 1964 car, stretched and restyled the body. The rear fenders were lengthened and squared off, while the front end was made a bit more bulky, but in a pleasing way. It looked like a more expensive product. The glamour cars were again highlighted in the brochures, both the convertible and the hardtop, and V-8 availability was shouted out. The new 327 cid Rambler V-8 was available, as was the 232 cid engine that had debuted the year before on the Typhoon.

For 1965, the Ambassador was "totally new in size, in style, in power!" The brochure stated, "You've never seen anything like it." That was certainly true; the public had never seen anything like it at all. The 1965 Ambassador was showing off a complete restyle that earned mixed reviews. The wheelbase was stretched to 116 inches in line with what the Big Three were doing, and its lines were squared, creating a handsome and stylish profile nearly identical to the new Classic. The front

102

end redesign chosen by Teague was something else again. In a move curiously similar to what was done with the 1961 Ambassador, the front end of the '65 was made to look as different as possible from the Classic to separate them in the buyer's mind. It did do that, just as it had in 1961. Although it looks odd today with its quad headlights stacked on top of each other, it sold pretty well in 1965, as Ambassador production zoomed to 64,145 units, the highest ever. Still, that 64,000 units was not much when the cost of tooling was considered. The Ambassador now had its own front end styling and a longer wheelbase, and all that cost money to tool for. In order to earn a fair profit, given that kind of expenditure, sales would have to be much higher.

The convertible was a new addition to the Ambassador line for 1965.

Sales of the Rambler Classic were down again, and the new Rambler American started to falter in the market. Abernethy took all this as a sign that he was on the right track in moving up-market as the lower-priced cars were the ones suffering the sales decreases. What he failed to realize was that he was essentially pitching the Rambler Ambassador to a new market now, reaching for the more conventional Big Three-type customer, and thus was increasing his sales of that one high-dollar line. He was also abandoning his traditional customers who had never really taken to the Ambassador and now were being turned off by the changes in the Classic. That owner base was the backbone of American Motors' successes, a loyal if somewhat eccentric band of conservative buyers.

Top: Handsome new styling was featured for the 1965 Ambassador. Bottom: The Classic had new styling and a new convertible model.

The 1965 Rambler American was popular with young families.

Unfortunately, Abernethy was walking away from his owner base as he tried to win new customers in a part of the market that had the most competition. The domestic Big Three was selling standard size cars for decades, had a cost structure that allowed them to build large cars at low costs, and had owner loyalty that would be hard to convert. The Big Three automakers had an image with the public as "big car" guys, whereas Rambler's image was well established as a builder of economical transportation. Rambler could look ahead and see increased competition in its end of the market, but at least there it would be fighting in a market it knew well, and with its cost structure in place and well understood. Its profits might get squeezed a bit if it remained a builder of small cars, but its reputation would probably always keep the wolf away from the door.

Of course, that's not what happened. Abernethy was a big car guy and had always been. To his credit, he had done a splendid job in the past, pushing his dealer body to greater and greater success. Now that he was in charge of the whole company, he decided to change things to the way he felt they should be. The course Abernethy chose nearly ran AMC into bankruptcy.

The handsome line of 1965 Ramblers represented the further change in image that Abernethy desired. The American, Classic and Ambassador were certainly completely different from even as recent as 1963. They now offered, as the brochure declared, "3 different sizes of cars, 3 different wheelbases, 7 spectacular powerplants!" And they were all offered under the collective slogan, "The Sensible Spectaculars."

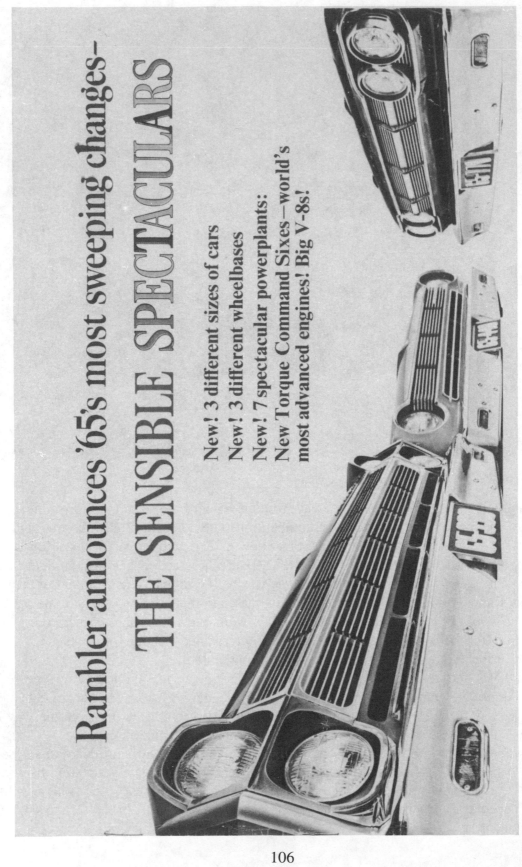

Rambler announces '65's most sweeping changes–
THE SENSIBLE SPECTACULARS

New! 3 different sizes of cars
New! 3 different wheelbases
New! 7 spectacular powerplants:
New Torque Command Sixes—world's
most advanced engines! Big V-8s!

"The sensible spectaculars": 1965's advertising theme was quite different from past Rambler advertising.

Different even when it was new - the Marlin.

The trouble was they didn't sell spectacularly. When the model year ended, a total of 412,736 Ramblers was sold worldwide. Even the addition of convertible models in the Classic and Ambassador lines, a first for AMC, had not helped. Collectively, only 8,452 were built, not enough to cover their costs. The Ambassador base series, the 880 models, were now offered in six- or eight-cylinder models, the first time the Ambassador had offered a six-cylinder since 1956. Now, since the Classic series offered an eight and the Ambassador a six-cylinder, the differences in the two cars had to be made up in the body rather than the power train. That was an expensive way to do things.

The Tarpon prototype evolved into the Marlin, only on a larger Classic chassis.

Profits for 1965 sank again, and this time the drop was serious. Net profit was $5,205,572, a fraction of the total of the year prior and the smallest profit American Motors had ever made. Net sales dropped below the billion mark, $990,618,709. And the all important working capital balance took an equally sharp plunge, down to $84,326,635, as tooling costs were not being offset by increased car sales. In the annual report, it was noted that results reflected lower sales and a strike in the fourth quarter that had shut down the Kenosha plant for three weeks. That had certainly hurt profits badly and would hurt sales in the 1966 model year, as the fourth quarter build was all 1966 models. But it did not explain the huge drop in sales of the 1965 models. Clearly, things were not going well and were getting worse.

The full range of models now offered were not selling at the level that the simple 1963 line had

Dick Teague designed this Tarpon sports coupe on the American's 106-inch wheelbase.

sold, and because they shared fewer parts among each other, were more expensive to build. The solution was to either increase sales of the range or go back to the original plan of sharing tooling to reduce costs. That would take several years to accomplish, as the entire range was redesigned and those bills still had to be amortized. Would it be easier than trying to increase sales of a line of cars that was beginning to be called, in whispered tones, failures? Some men would say yes, swallow hard and try to get the boat turned back around. Some men, particularly men who spent their lives in sales, might believe it easier to sell their way out of a bad fix, maybe even risk a further revamping of the lineup. A clue as to how Roy Abernethy felt could be found at the local Rambler dealer in February 1965 as a mid-year introduction was made of the all-new sporty fastback AMC car. This new Marlin, AMC said, was a look at the new direction the company was going. It most certainly was, unfortunately.

The 1965 Marlin represented one of the biggest product goofs that American Motors ever made. In response to the lithe, sensual new Mustang, AMC brought out the Marlin. Designer Dick Teague had introduced a concept car in 1964 called the Tarpon, built on the American's wheelbase, which offered a reasonable response to the Mustang. It was compact, a fastback, and it could have been sold at a low enough price to attract some plus sales volume. Its elliptical side windows were irritating to look at, and its stock American front end looked out of place, but it still could have sold in fair numbers. Responses from the public that saw it at auto shows were generally positive.

But when Abernethy viewed the prototype, he ordered it redesigned on the longer and larger Classic chassis to make it an intermediate sports car. Teague later reported that while he was in Europe, Abernethy ordered the roofline of the new larger car raised one inch. Teague felt this ruined the styling. The combination of a swoopy rear window with a narrow and poorly executed boat tail tagged

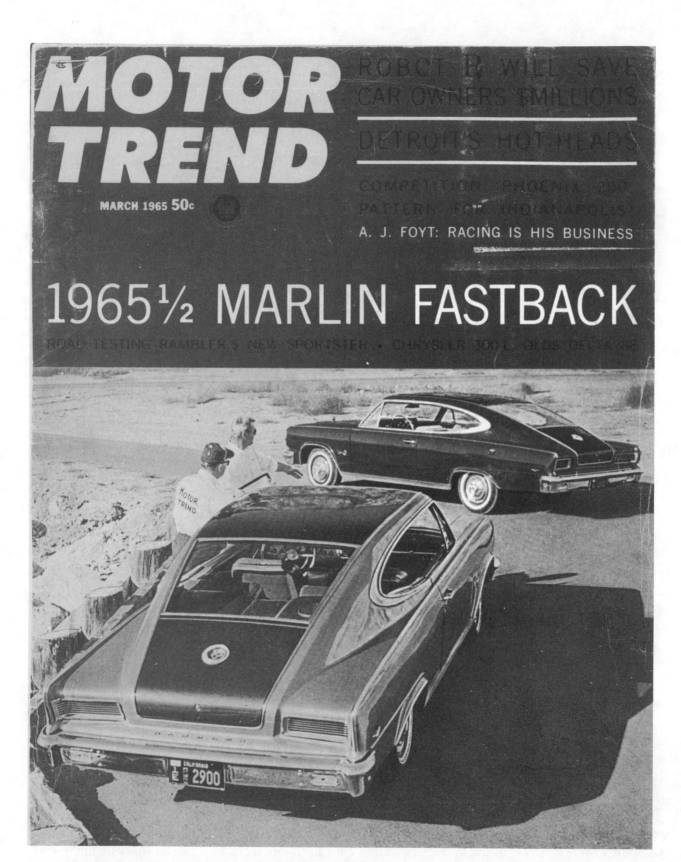

Motor Trend featured the Marlin on its cover of the March 1965 issue.

onto the flat square front end of the Rambler Classic was just too much of a mishmash. The Marlin sold 10,327 units for 1965. It's interesting to note that the very similar, though much better looking Dodge Charger of 1966 also flopped on the market as sporty car buyers were showing their preference for compact pony cars. That was the market AMC should have been in if it had to get into the sporty car market at all.

Most distressing was the announcement by Abernethy that beginning in 1966, the higher-priced models in the line, Ambassador and Marlin, would now be badged as individual makes and would not be Ramblers. In that one move, Abernethy was throwing out all the effort that had been expended since 1954 to consolidate to the Rambler nameplate. The 1963 cars were the first all-Rambler lineup, and now for 1966 that strategy was abandoned. Abernethy felt that continued association with the Rambler name was hurting sales of his big, expensive cars. Surely, this move would make 1966 a turnaround year.

Ambassador for 1966.

The move to the higher price ranges continued at AMC in 1966. The Ambassador line added a new DPL hardtop, plush and pretty. To make the point that this was a luxury hardtop, throw pillows matching the seat fabric were available. Cruise control was a new option, and station wagons were showing off a new wood side treatment. The Marlin, like the Ambassador, was no longer a Rambler model but was registered simply as a Marlin. The nameplate was the biggest change on the Marlin as it was a mostly carryover line.

The Rambler Classic came in for some changes, mostly good ones. The hardtop received a new, squarer roofline that looked nice and improved rear headroom as well. The new hardtop was called the Rambler Rebel, but unlike the 1957 or 1958 Rebel, it was to connote the top line body style and not a complete series of automobiles. The 1966 Classics had few other appearance changes as the big money was spent on the restyling done for 1965.

For 1966, Rambler American sported new front end styling.

The 1966 Rambler American now received a face-lift, a new set of front fenders (longer than the previous year), new hood, and new grille. The lengthened front end was a treat for it seemed to balance the lines of the American just right. Gone was the stubby nose and tunneled headlamps, though the latter appeared on other AMC products in the future. The new grille was a non-descript horizontal bar unit, though deeper than the prior year's.

A new model in the American series was the Rogue, a wistful name for an economy compact, but Abernethy was reaching for the top of the market in each segment now. The Rogue series was better trimmed and carried more standard equipment. This was presented to the consumer as a sporty compact, and indeed the Rogue received a larger base engine, the 232 cid in-line six. Also new in the American series was the availability of V-8 power for the first time. The new AMC 290 cid V-8 engine fit right into the engine bay of the American and provided performance that was most definitely not Ramblerlike. Four on the floor was now available as well, although only on the eight-cylinder cars.

Problems became apparent very quickly. While the new American was restyled, it was also priced directly against the Ford and Chevrolet compacts. Maybe that's where it belonged, but the Rambler image was starting to get fuzzy, and the American no longer had a lock on the compact car market. This change in AMC's image and philosophy was unfortunately having a disastrous effect on sales. The problem was compounded by the expense of the tooling invested in the cars. American Motors was now spending very large amounts of money to style each line differently, and that cost was preventing it from lowering its prices to reach out and bring in the buyers. The public was just not buying AMC's cars at the prices the company now needed to charge.

None of this should reflect badly on Dick Teague. Teague's redesigned 1964 American had sold well at first and had set a sales record. His 1965 Rambler Classic was a handsome and clever face-lift of an existing car. The 1965 Ambassador sold a bit better, but its styling was controversial and

112

probably turned off more prospective buyers than it turned on.

In a move that must have irritated the now retired Ed Anderson, Teague was promoted to vice president of styling in 1964, evidence of Abernethy's satisfaction with the 1964 American. Teague thus began a long career as the head of AMC styling.

Regardless of what Abernethy or anyone else believed would happen, 1966 American Motors cars sold very poorly in the marketplace. Production of the American, even with its new front styling and V-8 availability, dropped to under 100,000, a big drop from the 163,000 units built in 1964. The Rambler Classic also suffered a drop in sales. The Ambassador, which had seen 64,000 units built in 1965 and needed to at least double that number to pay its amortization costs, instead sold fewer, as less than 35,000 were built. Even the odd Marlin, which sold a bit over 10,000 cars in the short 1965 model year, dropped to a pathetic 4,547 units, silencing any boosters who held out hope that it could be a vibrant success.

Contrary to histories that have appeared before, where it is explained that the 1966 sales drop was only in the low-priced Rambler series, in truth the entire lineup of AMC cars sold poorly in 1966. Part of the "low-price sales drop" explanation can be described as wishful thinking by those in the company who championed the move to an expanded lineup.

The truth was difficult to face. AMC cars were being set upon by the worse detractor that can appear in the marketplace: rumor. It actually started with the sales decline of 1964, although it's hard to see it there. When sales had declined in 1964, Abernethy became more aggressive rather than more cautious and had pushed through a new product program that yielded the 1965 Classic/ Ambassador and the Marlin. The Marlin was a bad mistake, and it caused a loss of some image to be sure. But what hurt worst was the huge expense for new model tooling. At the rate Abernethy was spending money, there was little chance to earn a decent profit in 1965. When that tiny 1965 profit was noted by the press, they began to preface statements about AMC with distressful words, such as "struggling," "strapped," "financially ailing," and worse. That kind of talk then began to snowball.

By 1966, what were whispered words of discouragement began to be loud accusations of product deficiency. That kind of talk is deadly in the car market, as American Motors soon found out. To a public simply in the market for a new automobile, AMC didn't seem like the place to shop in 1966. After all, the company was losing money and could go out of business as Studebaker had done (and Studebaker finally did quit the car business in early 1966). The cars themselves didn't really offer anything that a person couldn't get on a Chevy, Mercury, Ford, or Pontiac. AMC's image was fuzzy now, too. They were still, at least they said, "The Economy King." But they were also "luxury" and "sporty" now. They were also in several market niches, and the whole thing was confusing to the customer. It could all be sorted out and made perfectly clear to the buyer if only several years and gigantic sums of money were invested in an advertising program to reeducate the customer. But AMC was fast running out of those two most precious commodities, time and money.

It was hoped the buff magazines would be rooting for the new performance emphasis at AMC, but it didn't turn out that way. Here again, American Motors was trying to pit its recent image change from family car to hot rod against the super-macho image of cars like the Pontiac GTO and Olds 442. AMC's small engineering staff tried to compete against competitors that were capable and willing to pump millions of dollars into their performance car image, even if it never paid back a profit. But little AMC didn't have the resources to play in that game for long, and when the losses from all this competition began to crowd the bottom line with red ink, it began to further erode the corporate image. By the end of 1966, the American Motors public image was that of a loser.

It's sad but true that all the problems were the result of some incorrect assumptions. Abernethy assumed that the buying public wanted another line of cars similar to what the Big Three already offered. In that regard, history has proven him wrong, for although his bigger models sold for a time, they soon fell into a sales slump. He also assumed that if the public liked the little Mustang, they would love an even bigger sporty car like the Marlin, and he was wrong on that count. He assumed that the buyers were no longer interested in plain economy models like the Rambler American and Classic, quality cars that offered real, lasting value rather than mere flashy style. Anyone who still held onto the belief that the image change was a correct plan that might have worked, given more time, should have looked to sales of the Volkswagen in the same time period, for Volkswagen was on a roll, selling more cars each year with no ceiling in sight.

But the single most important fatal assumption was that the best place for American Motors to compete was directly against the Big Three. History was certainly clear on that point, for just a few years prior, the Kaiser-Fraser company had learned the hard way what would happen to any independent automaker bold enough to challenge the market leaders on their own turf. Kaiser-Fraser, despite large capital resources, modern plants, modern and plush products, and a product launch in the middle of a seller's market, crashed and died within a decade. The old line Studebaker Corporation just fizzled out. And, of course, the best example was AMC itself, which was forged in adversity, remade into a niche marketer, and founded its success on remaining in market segments below the American standard-size car. The end result of ignoring history could be guessed at.

It was all summed up in the annual report for 1966, a document that must have startled any longtime AMC stockholders. The report itself is noteworthy by its use of a plain paper cover instead of the glossy full-color covers of previous years. In the struggling years of 1956, 1957 and 1958, the

Hope for the future: AMX, Vignale prototytpe, was one of the Project IV idea cars.

114

annual reports were similarly stark in design. The use of such low cost materials for the report indicated at a glance that things were not good, and costs were being cut everywhere.

The numbers inside were very bad. Sales had slipped again, the third year in a row, to $870,449,056, a drop of $120 million from 1965. This time the company slid into a net loss of $12,648,170. This was bad enough, but the operating loss was really a total of $30,918,170, which was reduced by an income tax credit of $15,200,000. Net working capital was down again to $52,789,549, quite a drop from the $125 million of 1963. Worldwide wholesale sales of American Motors cars dropped to 345,886 compared with 412,736 in 1965. Domestic sales were the ones that suffered, as the drop there was to 271,466 from 1965's 338,176.

Abernethy's American Motors was in a tailspin, and he and the company began to frantically search for a way out of its troubles. The chairman of the board, Richard Cross, was replaced by the largest stockholder, Robert B. Evans. Evans planned to get the company back on track again and soon. Cross was almost a ceremonial figure as Abernethy ran the auto business. One retired AMC

The Cavalier was another Project IV design using cross-interchangeable doors. Fender shapes and wheel openings predicted the styling of the 1970 Hornet.

executive opined that Cross was made vice chairman only to keep the seat warm for George Romney in the event his bid for the governorship of Michigan failed.

Evans was also inexperienced in the auto business, but was highly opinionated and determined to at least head AMC in the right direction. Evans was also willing to try new ideas and was a strong believer in new product directions.

Abernethy himself was trying new ideas. It was announced that the 1967 lineup "represents the fruition of this continuing program of investment in the future, and puts American Motors into a new, wider ranging area of consumer appeal." Much more important, near the end of the 1966 model year, Roy D. Chapin Jr., son of one of the founders of Hudson Motor Car Company and the architect of Rambler's success in the overseas market, was made executive vice president and automotive general manager. Chapin had been in the upper ranks of American Motors management since its founding and held various jobs, all of which he had done well. Now, based on his success overseas and finally realizing that the company was unraveling, Chapin was given control of all automotive

Top: Rambler Rogue hardtop for 1967. Bottom: Though still looking good, the 1967 American convertible sold poorly.

activities.

There was a wholesale reshuffling of executives, all in a move to reignite sales. At the behest of both Abernethy and Evans, work was begun on still more new products. A special touring group of protoype cars, called Project IV, was sent to various cities to both gauge public reaction to new concept automobiles and to try to regain the confidence of stockbrokers and the press. Hopes were pinned on the newly redesigned production cars that, with luck, would sell well enough to halt the sales slide of 1964-1966 and give the company breathing room until radically new cars, like the Project IV vehicles, could be rushed to market. With a prayer for luck, Abernethy and American Motors began the 1967 model year. It was to be a critical year in the life of the company.

The 1967 Rambler Rebel was a very handsome design that failed to sell in volume. Top: Rebel station wagon. Bottom: Rambler Rebel SST convertible.

Sporty 1967 Rebel hardtop on the new 114-inch wheelbase.

Anyone looking for a sleeper, a hot car waiting to be discovered, didn't find it at their American Motors dealer in the fall of 1966 when the 1967 AMC cars were introduced. The little Rambler American was back for another year, wearing its same basic styling but jazzed up with further new options and colors. The lineup of Americans was smaller now, a base 220 series that included a two-door sedan, four-door sedan and station wagon. The 440 series was the next step up, and included the same body styles plus a hardtop. The Rogues were available as a two-door hardtop or convertible.

The Rambler Classic was gone, replaced by a new series called the Rebel. The Rebel nameplate was, of course, an old one at AMC and had just been used on the prior year's top-line Classic model, but for 1967 it was used on a completely redesigned line of cars. These new Rebels were Ramblers, but advertising deliberately downplayed that association. Even in the brochures for the year the Rambler name is scarcely used.

These were handsome cars, built on a new, longer 114-inch wheelbase. The line began with a low priced two-door sedan called the Rebel 550 series, which featured very slim "B" pillars to give a hardtop look. The 550 line additionally held a four-door sedan and a low-priced wagon. The next series was the 770, which had the four-door sedan and station wagon like the 550 series but had a true pillarless hardtop two-door instead of the psuedo hardtop of the cheaper line. The top of the all-new Rebel series was the Rebel SST, available as a two-door hardtop or convertible. The full range of power and convenience options were available as well as a wide choice of engines on all the Rebel models. Styling was so good that Dodge used the same theme for its Coronet line the following year.

Smoother styling on the 1967 Ambassador failed to ignite sales as AMC faced the "dark days of 1967."

The Ambassador series held a number of good-looking cars as well, as they also carried the new styling theme. Long and wide, the slab styling echoed that of the 1967 Oldsmobiles, at least in profile and when viewed from the rear. Up front the Ambassador carried a new version of Teague's quad headlamps, which for this year were tunneled into the fenders as well as stacked. The all-new Ambassador lineup for 1967 had the usual two-door hardtop and two-door convertible in the top line DPL trim, as well as 990 series two-door hardtop, four-door sedan and station wagon, and a lower-

Complete failure: The 1967 Marlin, now built on the Ambassador chassis, sold in small numbers.

priced 880 series with a four-door station wagon, sedan and the two-door slim pillar sedan body shared with the Rebel. A new model in the Ambassador range was the Marlin hardtop. After sales went from poor in 1965 to lousy in 1966, Abernethy decided to move the car still further upmarket in an attempt to position it where there was no competition at all. The move to the Ambassador range was costly, as it required new tooling, and all these tooling bills were sinking the company.

The hoopla got louder in 1967, and the sales message now seemed to be shrill with a tone of desperation in it. The Rebels, the public was told, were the "Excitement Machines." The Ambassadors, said the brochures, offered "four on the floor and three in the rear," the latter referring to the

1967 Ambassador DPL hardtop.

William V. Luneburg, president, American Motors Corporation.

improved rear seat room. Ambassadors were "luxury cars created for today." And Marlin? "Marlin is totally new, poised on its new 118-inch wheelbase, Marlin is six inches longer, almost four inches wider ... there's plenty of room for six swingers." Swingers? Well, after all, this was 1967.

The all-new Ambassadors, swinging new Marlins and sharp new Rebels didn't turn the trick in 1967. It was pretty obvious to Robert Evans that things were not going right. A meeting of the board of directors was called in January 1967, when finances became so tight that there was some doubt about the company's ability to last to the end of the model run in summer.

At the board meeting on Jan. 9, 1967, options were discussed among the members. Included were Bob Evans, Roy Abernethy, Roy Chapin and most of the board of directors. After a time, it was decided that a change of management was the only hope for the company. In a vote it was decided that Roy D. Chapin Jr. would become the new chairman of the board and chief executive officer, and that William V. Luneburg would be president and chief operating officer.

Robert Evans stayed on as a director, but Abernethy, president since 1962, was forced to retire. His legacy at American Motors was a mixed one at best. His early successes working under Romney were instrumental in holding the fragile dealer network together in the worst of times, and he had reworked that weakened group into a strong and profitable sales channel that set records for sales that remain unbeaten today. His inability to recognize the danger of a frontal attack on the Big Three

121

remains as one of history's great riddles, for he most certainly knew the nature of the automobile business. Perhaps he felt that he would be the one to beat the odds, just as Henry Kaiser had once felt.

Of more immediate concern to Chapin and Luneburg was the financial mess with which they were left. Cash was running out, costs were climbing and a glut of unsold new cars was clogging dealer lots and, worse yet, the storage yards at American Motors. It was, as Chapin would recall later, "the dark days of 1967." Some things needed immediate attention, such as the cash crunch. Looking over the figures, it was apparent that the corporation would be unable to meet its payroll in just a few weeks. This prompted what Chapin described as "some quick trips to our banks in New York." At meetings with the banks, terms were worked out to borrow money to meet operating expenses, but with conditions on a reasonable pay back of part of the debt in a short time. After sorting out the cash crunch, Chapin next put AMC's Redisco subsidiary on the market. Redisco (REfridgerator DIScount COmpany) was the finance arm of Kelvinator Appliances, the major AMC subsidiary that was a part of the company right from the beginning. Nash had bought Kelvinator many years prior just to gain the management services of Kelvinator's president, George Mason. Putting Redisco on the block was a difficult move for the company, but there was really no alternative, save for leaving the automobile business.

These were some of the 3,745 Ambassadors purchased by the U.S. Government for 1967. Most were used as postal vehicle.

For the entire year, dollar volume for the corporation continued its fall, now dropping to $778,009,192, down nearly $100 million from 1966. Worldwide wholesale unit sales of cars were just 291,090. The total included some 14,000 low profit units sold to rental car companies and 3,745 Ambassador sedans sold to the General Services Administration for use by the U.S. Postal Service. This latter sale was probably engineered by the government to give the company a quick cash infusion. These Ambassadors were painted medium blue with a white painted roof and door tops and have to go down in history as one of the best-looking postal vehicles of all time.

122

Top: The new AMC advertising agency. Left to right: Herbert Fisher, executive vice president, and Mary Wells, president of Wells, Rich, Greene, Inc. talk with Roy D. Chapin Jr. Bottom; New Javelin coming off the line at Kenosha, Wisconsin.

American Motors suffered a huge loss for 1967, $75,814,962. It was the worst loss in its history, a staggering amount for that decade. Roy Chapin worked in a whole range of write downs and losses into that, including $22,420,000 for unusual items such as write-off of tax benefits deferred in prior years, loss on the sale of Redisco, and revaluation of some foreign investments. It was the way Chapin liked to show things, and it made certain that there would be no surprises to bushwack the company in the future.

Finances took precedence in 1967 as Chapin struggled to gain control of the balance sheet. Borrowings increased mid-year to $95 million, then were reduced to $63,500,000 when proceeds from the sale of Redisco were received. A further payment brought down the bank debt to $60 million. Costs were attacked. Wages, salaries and benefits were cut by $15 million as the total number of employees dropped to 23,704 from 1966's total of 27,845. There were now 11,000 fewer employees at AMC than in 1963.

There was less working capital as well, as that balance dropped to only $35 million dollars. The picture presented was an ugly one, a company on the ropes. Yet Chapin and Luneburg had an air of quiet confidence as they calmly worked one-by-one through the many problems that faced the company. The biggest problem now was image, for in reality, AMC products were really quite attractive and represented good value and top-quality cars. But the public didn't know or care about that as they stayed away in droves, put off by the loser image. This was the paramount problem as Chapin and the board saw it, and Chapin moved fast to correct it. A new advertising company was signed, a youthful and creative firm called Wells, Rich, Greene Inc., and headed by Mary Wells. Wells, Rich, Greene Inc. was now charged with the mission of completely revamping the AMC public image, and as quickly as possible.

As Chapin explained to the stockholders, no changes could be contemplated in the product until 1970 as the product programs were locked in until then and could not be altered. Fortunately, a new car was coming for 1968 that would fit right in with the new, young, and winning image that AMC now planned to pursue. It was a compact sporty car, a pony car like the Mustang, and it was conceived and okayed for production during the brief reign of Bob Evans. The new car, called the Javelin, had a modest sales goal to achieve; just 35,000 units is all the company hoped for. If it could do that, it would be a success as the Marlin in its first year had sold less than a third of that number. The restyling of the Marlin as a full-size sporty car for 1967 proved what many people suspected. There was no competition in the full-size fastback market because there was no full-size fastback market! Only 2,545 1967 Marlins were sold. It would have been terribly funny if it had not been so costly to the company.

1967 goes down as the low point in American Motors history, a point when it would have been easy to give up and go out of business. 1968 would be the beginning of a slow and painful comeback as the new management team of Chapin and Luneburg took command.

As 1968 unfolded, it was apparent to many that a new spirit was taking hold at American Motors. The new management team seemed to be everywhere at once, visiting dealers to reassure them, holding press conferences to explain the company's new direction to the press, meeting with investors in New York to try to assuage their very real fears for the health of the company.

The product picture was very good for 1968. The new sporty Javelin generated great interest from the enthusiast magazines, creating tons of free advertising. The Rebel series was back mostly unchanged, but was now just plain Rebel as the Rambler nameplate was dropped on that line as well. The Ambassadors were getting a big share of the press, too, as air conditioning was made standard

1968 Ambassador hardtop.

equipment across the board on all Ambassadors. This move, suggested by marketing maven R. William McNealy, at least gave AMC something new to crow about on the holdover Ambassadors and was part of an overall effort to reposition the company as something new, a "consumerist" company. The little American was back, now the sole model with a Rambler nameplate.

The Rambler American line was trimmed for 1968. The low-price 220 line consisted of two-door and four-door sedans, no station wagons. The 440 line consisted of a four-door sedan and a four-door station wagon. The top-of-the-line was now the Rogue, available as a single two-door hardtop model. The convertible was dropped and the rest of the line trimmed to concentrate on the most popular models. Prices were cut the previous January, and sales improved. This led Chapin to believe the little Rambler was still a contender if it got back to its simple roots, and those roots fit in nicely with this new consumerist message that Wells, Rich, Greene Inc. was developing.

The base American 220 two-door sedan began at just $1946 for 1968, $315 less than the six-cylinder Chevy II.

The convertibles were cut from the Ambassador line as well, but in that instance it was only to be able to put emphasis on the new standard air conditioner while acknowledging that the convertible had never sold well and was a money loser. Since the new Javelin was planned only as a single coupe model, this meant that the Rebel series would be the only one left with a convertible. Not that this was a critical move, for the market for convertibles had shrunk badly and had proven to be an unprofitable one for AMC. The two-door sedans were cut from both the Rebel and Ambassador lines, which meant that the American was now the only two-door sedan at AMC. But a stripped 550 series convertible was added to the Rebel line to see if it could grab any extra sales.

The new look in advertising was subtle yet profound. The color catalogs still showed cars, but now the emphasis was on the cars and not on the people who showed them. In fact, in most pictures the cars were shown without accompanying actors and seemed to stand out more. The text was certainly less shrill and carried a somewhat irreverent tone to it. Gone were references to swingers, and in were plain, informative statements about the product. The pictures were big and the cars filled

Top: 1968 Rambler American station wagon. Bottom: 1968 Rambler Rogue offered hardtop styling and optional V-8 power.

them. The full model range was shown, with references and photos of the lowest-priced and more expensive series. The emphasis was put on the product and what it could provide for the customer in the way of value rather than image.

Straight talk and plain answers were the word of the day, as one tag line clearly shows: "Either we're charging too little, or everyone else is charging too much." It got one's attention and created a

Top: AMC designer Krispinsky penned this AMX study. Bottom: AMC designer Erich Kreigler drew this AMX study, showing "Ramble seat."

talking campaign among the public, talk that was favorable. Each car had a lead-in phrase that preceded the ad copy. For the new Javelin it was, "Its price is much less than Mustang's, yet you get much more." The Rebel's was, "It's the best dollar value in the automobile business." The American's was, "It's the only car made in America priced under $2,000." And Ambassador, of course, was, "The only American line of cars with air conditioning standard."

All of this was to create the value image that Chapin knew he needed. There could be no changing the product, at least not an extensive change, and at any rate, Chapin had come to realize an important truth: the Rambler image had taken such a hammering under the aegis of Abernethy that it would be impossible to rebuild the image while still using the Rambler name on anything save the lowest-priced cars. It was time, he knew, to begin to build a new image, different from the go-go days of 1965-1967 but similar to the value image the Rambler nameplate used to have. It was going

The boss' car - this was Dick Teague's personal AMX; it featured body colored bumpers, outside exhaust pipes and hood pins.

to have to be done without the Rambler name this time, as Rambler now connoted, at best, a cheap ride and, at worst, a car for losers.

Chapin was one of the catalysts who got the new Javelin into production. As he states, "I had practically begged Roy Abernethy to put the compact Tarpon into production back in 1964. I felt that the market wanted a compact sporty car, not a big one like the Marlin." So when Robert Evans asked him his opinion of the prototype Javelin, Chapin pushed to get the program going. It proved to be a wise move and also served as the platform for the most exciting AMC car of the decade, the AMX.

AMC Vice President of Marketing Services R.W. McNealy presents the keys to an all-pink 1968 AMX to Playboy magazine's "Playmate of the Year," Angela Dorian.

129

The change begins: The 1968 AMC Javelin began another change of image for AMC.

AMX was originally part of the Project IV show. Teague had wanted a specialty car that would really grab attention, and the one-off body, hand-built by Vignale of Italy, certainly was an eyepopper. When Evans began to push to get the AMX built, Teague modified the design so that it could be built in AMC's own Wisconsin plants instead of in Europe like the Nash-Healey. Teague planned for AMX to use a great deal of Javelin stampings both to make assembly easier and to cut tooling costs to a minimum. It worked like a charm, and AMX provided AMC with an ultra high-performance image car at just the right time, and at a budget that meant it could also be a money maker as well. The AMX was introduced on Feb. 24, 1968 as a mid-year model; 6,725 numbered editions were built for 1968. While that number didn't make a big difference on the profit statement, the importance of the AMX cannot be misunderstood. AMX was the symbol of a new American Motors, the rallying point for all the employees and dealers. The press coverage alone was worth millions of dollars, and it was all free. Dealers reported seeing a whole new group shopping at their agencies, a younger group that was impressed with the performance and appearance of the AMX and its Javelin cousin. These new shoppers, along with the newly excited auto press, began to turn the tide of public opinion about AMC. As Chapin said, "When we introduced the new Javelin, some

130

veteran dealers came up to me with tears in their eyes, they were so happy." Indeed, the dealers had seen the first flickering lights of their salvation.

So pleased was Chapin with the response to the AMX that he authorized the building of other AMX showcars and prototypes to keep the excitement level high.

The obscure AMX III prototype led to the Hornet Sportabout of 1971.

The sales strategy for the American was to concentrate on its low price, under $2,000, targeting it as an alternative to imported cars. It worked and worked well; American sales bounced back strongly. Rebels and Ambassadors fared a bit worse, but Javelin and AMX sales were over 60,000 combined, quite a bit more than the 35,000 AMC had hoped for.

Midway through 1968 it became apparent that more cash was needed to fund the redirected efforts of the company. The Kelvinator Division had always contributed to the company's profits, but it needed some cash reinvested in it to maintain its competitve position. Chapin instead decided to sell the division. This produced a paper loss of $10.8 million dollars on Kelvinator as it was sold for less than book value, but it provided AMC with cash and allowed AMC to focus its planning. American Motors was now a car company, period, and would live or die on car sales.

Sales did bounce back, somewhat, for 1968. Total worldwide wholesale sales were 322,742, of which about 268,000 were U.S. sales. Encouraging was the fact that the increase had all come in the vital U.S. market as international sales of AMC cars had dropped a bit. In the annual report, both

The 1968 Rambler 220 was low priced and reliable.

Renault Torino: Built in Argentina by Renault, Torino used a modified Rambler American body. This car was sold for over a decade as an expensive grand tourer.

1969 Rebel featured styling refinements.

Chapin and Luneburg wore wide, happy smiles, satisfied with the work they had done in their first full year in charge. Dollar sales for the year were down again, but that was because of the sale of Kelvinator and the subsequent loss of its revenue. Management instead highlighted dollar volume for the automotive end of the business to show a more accurate (and rosier) financial picture. Looking at just the auto business, which is all AMC would have now, income had risen by $110 million. There was an operating profit, a slim one for certain, but it was $4.8 million and it had come from selling cars. The company even had to pay income taxes. After receiving a special tax loss credit and accounting for the book loss on Kelvinator, the corporation was able to report net earnings of $11,761,828.

Although Chapin was an old Hudson man, he had the fiscal conservatism of George Mason and managed to jack the working capital balance up to $77,900,346, while paring the number of employees down to 21,338. Wages and benefits also fell to $202,852,627. Stockholders' equity rose, and it seemed as if the train was not only back on the track but also heading in the right direction. For 1969, Chapin budgeted for 300,000 U.S. car sales, which he felt AMC could reasonably hope to reach. And, as he stated in the annual report, AMC now had enough working capital to "take advantage of opportunities as they are developed." Roy Chapin had in mind a company he wanted to buy, but he was not prepared to pursue it until American Motors was out of the woods.

1969 AMX featured 140 mph speedometer and a leather seat option.

A slimmed down and reinvigorated American Motors began yet another year in the auto business. This was 1969, a new year, and the last year of the sixties. It was also the end of an era, for Chapin and the board decided that this would be the end of the line for the Rambler, the last year that grand old name would be used.

The product line for 1969 had really been decided by Roy Abernethy three years earlier when he was the top man. As Chapin said, there was no way to change the product, save changes to the way the product was marketed and sold. Javelin, AMX, and Rebel were all carryover models with

The AMX was built on a cut-down Javelin chassis.

Back for a curtain call, the 1969 Rambler.

changes in trim and equipment but no change in the basic body styling. The American nameplate was gone now as that car was rechristened simply the "Rambler." It was a way of letting people know that there was no longer a Rambler make while still retaining the name for use one last time on the lowest-priced car.

There were some noteworthy changes in the makeup of the Rambler line. Models were shuffled around to better serve demand for the true volume sellers. The base series was now called just Rambler with no 220 designation, while the middle series was still called the 440. The base series consisted of two- and four-door sedans, while the 440 series had a four-door sedan and station wagon. The two-door hardtop was back as the top-line Rogue series.

The AMC Ambassador wagon for 1969 offered a new dual-swing tailgate.

The big news for 1969 was the Ambassador. One of Abernethy's last moves was to authorize an increase in size for the big Ambassador to firmly plant it in the largest car category. The plans were far along when he exited the company, so AMC, like it or not, was to have a big new Ambassador to sell in 1969. This was not just a bigger car, it was the biggest Ambassador ever! Still, Wells, Rich, Greene Inc. hit on the correct way to merchandise the Ambassador, showing off its increased size and all-out luxury while still using a value pitch. The unifying theme for Ambassador was near genius in tying luxury and value together in one simple statement: "It will remind you of the days when money really bought something." With its new 122-inch wheelbase and sharp styling by Dick Teague, this was as handsome a car as you could hope for, and it was solid and comfortable, available in two-door hardtop, four-door sedan or station wagon. The trim levels were now called basic,

The 1969 Ambassador was the biggest Ambassador ever.

1969 SC/Rambler, a.k.a. the Hurst Rambler. Note the striped headrests and 390 V-8 badges.

DPL, and top-line SST. The 232 cid six was standard on the base and DPL, and air conditioning was still standard on all Ambassadors. Interestingly, the hood line carried a strong theme, shaped to give an image of a classic radiator shell and giving a hint of the cusps that were trademarks of the Packard. After all, Teague was the last head of Packard styling in Detroit, so maybe it wasn't just coincidental.

In retrospect, it was not the strongest lineup, but it was felt that the cars would do well now that the public and press had witnessed the turnaround. After all, it was not the product that had caused the sales drop in the first place. The losses were merely the end result of overspending on tooling for new models. That overspending made it impossible to earn a profit. The lack of profit began a flood of negative publicity that caused a further fall off in sales, the result of which was a downward tailspin. But now that costs were getting under control, reasonable profits could be had even with a slight downturn in sales and could really mushroom with a slight sales upturn.

Midway through the year the company decided to have a little fun and further its gutsy "comeback kid" image. A limited production specialty car was cobbled up by fitting AMC's biggest engine, the AMX 390 cid V-8, into the smallest car, the 106-inch wheelbase Rambler (nee American). With performance rear axle gears and four on the floor gearbox, the SC/Rambler accelerated like a sidewinder missile. Painted in white with high profile red and blue accents and sporting styled wheels and fat tires, it got attention on the street. AMC wisely priced it low at $2,998. It was not

138

meant to sell in volume nor be a profit center. Instead, it was to be an image maker, a car that the press would write stories about and keep AMC in the news. Because it used existing tooling and hardware, it would be very cost effective. The program would pay for itself even at the planned volume of only 500 units. But when it hit the market, demand was far higher than anyone, even the optimistic Chapin, had expected. A second batch of 500 units was built, and then a final 512 more, for a total of 1,512 SC/Ramblers. Variously referred to as Scrambler Ramblers, SCs, or Hurst Ramblers, these wonderful cars remain as perhaps the most collectible AMC cars of the sixties.

AMX GT: This photo shows the prototype with wind-cheating aero wheel covers and blackwall tires.

AMC was also showing off a prototype AMX GT, or Grand Tourer, and it was something to see. This new show car had a short 97-inch wheelbase and a truncated body that ended just aft of the rear wheels in a severely chopped hatchback. The press and public alike were lukewarm to the shape, and AMC had no plans to pursue the idea as a production AMX model. But designer Teague had sprung the AMX GT onto the auto show crowds as a way of preparing them for the radical products he had designed for the decade of the seventies.

Things didn't turn out like they were supposed to in 1969. The lineup of cars didn't experience any dramatic upturn, and as a matter of record actually turned down a bit. Worldwide unit sales came in at 309,334. Dollar volume for the company was $737,449.000, not like the old days and off some $24 million from 1968. Costs were being driven up by the expense of tooling for an all-new

AMX GT: Shown in 1968 as an AMX prototytpe, the basic styling predicted the Gremlin of 1970.

range of cars planned for the 1970 model year. Despite all that, a profit was eeked out, only $4,928,000, but it was a real profit, coming from operations and not from the sale of assets. Obviously, the corporation couldn't expect to survive for many years on a slim diet of profits like that, and Chapin was concerned.

At this point Chapin was between a rock and a very hard place. The money he had invested in new products would pay him back handsomely, he felt. But he also felt it would be just a touch too late for him to utilize those anticipated profits to purchase a company he was watching for some time now, like a cat watching a fish bowl. Kaiser Corporation, current owner of the old Willys Overland, was tired of the auto business and wanted to get out of it. Its own brand, Kaiser, had died in the market in the fifties. Kaiser had bought out Willys Overland in that decade, renamed it Kaiser Jeep in the sixties, and had a mixed run in the market. By 1969 Kaiser knew that competition would continue to grow in the four-wheel-drive market, and that more cash would have to be invested in Jeep to keep it competitive. It had already been showing a prototype of a four-wheel-drive sports car, called XJ001, at various auto shows to gauge reaction. The vision of increased cost and increased competition made Kaiser decide to seek a buyer for Jeep, someone who was more interested in the auto business than it was itself. Roy Chapin sent one of his most trusted aides, Gerry Meyers, to look over the Kaiser Jeep plants. What Meyers saw was a mixed bag of old rundown plants in Toledo, Ohio building civilian Jeeps, and a modern factory in South Bend, Indiana building government destined vehicles. The Indiana plant was purchased just a few years earlier from the Studebaker Corporation when it had shut down all U.S. manufacturing. Meyers did a detailed study and advised Roy Chapin that his recommendation was to pass up any plans to buy Jeep.

On June 30, 1969, the last Rambler ever to be built in America came down the final assembly line

The end of the Rambler - the 1969 Rambler four-door.

in Kenosha, Wisconsin. Some longtime workers paused to be photographed with the historic vehicle. From 1950 to 1969, 4,204,925 Ramblers were built, and this was the last one. Soon, a new model year would begin, and then the start of a new calendar year. This would also be the start of a new decade, the first decade in history when there would be just one independent automaker left to offer the American public something different from the Big Three. What would the decade of the seventies offer to a still struggling independent like AMC?

Chapter 4

1970-1973
A New Division and a New Chance

There are a few pat sayings concerning growth and progress, one of which is the familiar "you have to spend money to make money," and that was certainly true of American Motors in 1970. Another saying that was too true was "no pain, no gain."

It was a busy year in the life of the corporation, almost a dizzying year in fact. As the last few days of 1969 played out, the new 1970 AMC cars were introduced to the market. The expected though lamented name change became complete as the Rambler brand name was dropped forever. From 1950 to 1969, a 20-year period, Rambler had been a prominent name in the American automobile market, indeed was the only reason why there still was an American Motors Corporation, but it had been irreversibly harmed by the Abernethy years, and now it was time to lay it to rest.

Its handsome replacement was now being looked over by the press and the public and for the most part, it was deemed a worthy successor. The 1970 AMC Hornet was an attempt to meld the frugal image of the Rambler with an image of luxury into a new type of compact car. As *Car and Driver* magazine noted, "... Chapin has shown that he understands the essential difference between small cars and economy cars. Mavericks and Volkswagens are economy cars. The Hornet is a small car."

The Hornet was more modern looking, for certain, but after all, the last Rambler had been on the market since 1964 with only a mild face-lift, so anything would look newer than that. The important change was to be how the car was merchandised, packaged. AMC was taking a few lessons from the original Ford Mustang of 1965 to properly market its new little car.

The new Hornet was designed by Dick Teague and was to be the basis of a whole new group of car lines. The program was very nearly a copy of George Romney's shared chassis program, although updated to meet the marketing realities of the 1970s. The 1970 Hornet was offered in sedans only, a two-door and a four-door. Built on a 108-inch wheelbase, the new sedans had a long

Out with the old and in with the new: The Hornet, on a 108-inch wheelbase, was the new compact for a new decade and replaced the Rambler for 1970.

hood/short rear deck styling theme that was in line with public tastes of the time. The long hood/ short deck design was usually seen in sporty cars like the Mustang/Javelin pony cars, but its basic elements had been used in 1969 for the new Ford Maverick compact car, which had proven to be an immensely popular product. Since the new Hornet was going to be forced to compete against the Maverick, it was decided to use that information when designing the Hornet and use a longer wheelbase to ensure a roomier interior than the Ford.

In order to sell in the volume needed, the Hornet was offered in two trim levels, base and SST. This marked the first use of the SST trim designation on the lowest priced AMC products and was a part of the attempt to drive home the idea that the Hornet was a new concept in small cars ... a luxury compact. Base cars were equipped similarly to the way the basic Rambler had been: stripped down. The lowest-priced models came with rubber floor mats instead of carpeting, vinyl bench seats, hubcaps instead of wheel discs -- just the basics -- while the SST models had carpeting, cloth seats, and better trim. The standard engine on the base Hornet was the 199 cid six carried over from the Rambler. The SST got the bigger 232 cid six as standard. Both of these engines were modern seven main bearing designs that featured smoothness unmatched by any other domestic car, and they delivered excellent fuel economy and long service life.

The Hornet was meant to be profitable when sold in stripped down form, but the big profits were going to come from the sale of options. In a move similar to how the original Mustang was merchandised, Hornet was offered with an option list that was long and varied. Besides the two six-cylinder

143

The Gremlin was introduced on April 1, 1970. Newsweek featured the car on the cover of its April 6, 1970 issue.

engines mentioned, an optional two-barrel version of the 232 was available, as was a 304 cid V-8. Shift Command automatic transmission was a very popular option, and so were the reclining seats, power steering and brakes (disc or drum), air conditioning, electric clock, pin stripes, vinyl roof, choice of wheel covers, and more. It was a range of options that was rare for the time, at least in the low-price field, and even surpassed what Abernethy had offered in prior years.

Looked at that way, it seems that the old mistakes of the Abernethy years were just being rescrambled and served up again, and that this diversity of offerings would drive AMC's costs out of sight. But the Hornet program had been carefully conceived and watched over by men like Teague, Chapin, Meyers, and Luneburg, men who had survived corporate collapse before and knew how to avoid it again. The Hornet design itself was a clever use of shared stampings. Unnoticed by the press, the two-doors and four-doors shared the same roof stampings and had bumpers that interchanged front to rear. These two features had been designed by Dick Teague and represented a savings of millions of dollars in tooling while simultaneously saving factory space, inventory costs, and labor. Lessons in tool sharing had been learned from the 1963 program of Ed Anderson and George Romney and had been honed by Teague with his Cavalier concept car. Looking at the Cavalier, it's easy to see where the Hornet got its styling. The 108-inch wheelbase chassis was planned to be the foundation for other new products as well. A station wagon was definitely in the works for 1971 and a new pickup truck, based on the Hornet, was even now being cobbled together in the prototype shops. Called the Cowboy, it might bring in a whole new group of customers.

It is interesting to note that a two-door hardtop was not offered, nor was a convertible, as those two models were very expensive to tool, and AMC had learned the hard way that those two body styles were just not profitable in the lower end of the market. It was more cost effective to offer wide ranging choices on the option list instead of in the range of body styles. That was the strength of this new model program. A wide array of options and various trim would allow a shopper to custom tailor his or her car to his or her own tastes. But unlike the bad old days, the hard costs, that is, body tooling, would be held to a minimum.

This new program didn't come cheap. AMC spent $40 million designing and tooling for the Hornet. It was planned to be the lead product in AMC's attempt to sell a compact car in large volume. The Rambler American, while selling at a profitable rate in the late sixties, had been a disappointment in that it failed to sell in very high volume, except for in 1964 when the newly redesigned American had made its debut. It was felt by Chapin and Luneberg that AMC should be taking a much larger share of the market below the intermediate size, as that was the area in which AMC specialized. Since $40 million had been invested in this new car, it would simply have to sell in volume in order for it to be a profit maker. With the Hornet as his lead product, Roy Chapin now planned to, as he put it, "introduce a new product every six months," at least until he got volume up to the level he wanted.

The next product came out on April Fool's Day 1970, and it surprised a lot of people. The Gremlin was the first American-built subcompact car, at least from a major maker. Badged as the AMC Gremlin, it rode a wheelbase of just 96 inches, four inches less than the original Rambler of 1950. The subcompact market had been left to the imports prior to 1970, but it was recognized as a segment that was growing rapidly and it was thought to be an important area for growth throughout the seventies. General Motors and Ford were still putting the finishing touches on their new entries in this segment, so the Gremlin beat the Chevy Vega and Ford Pinto to market by a full six months. It was not an important victory volumewise, for the Gremlin sold only a moderate amount of cars in that slim time frame, but it was an important image boost for AMC as a whole and served as fair warning that AMC was now prepared to fight all out for a bigger share of the small car market. It also showed the world, including the all important press, that AMC had the capability to outgun the Big Three in certain areas.

Anybody with a ruler and at least one good eye could readily see where the Gremlin had come from and why it got to market so fast. The Gremlin's chassis was a shortened Hornet chassis, cut down by one foot. The front fenders and doors were shared with the Hornet, along with the windshield, front bumper, and most of the dash. The hood was nearly identical and could be stamped on the same press. The only body tooling needed was for the two rear quarter panels, roof, rear valance, and a modified floor pan. Seats and interior trim were mostly from the Hornet, and the cars were built on the new Hornet assembly line as well. This bit of wizardry worked magic on the tooling budget, as it was reported in the press that the cost of tooling the Gremlin was just $6 million. The base engine on the Gremlin was the 199 cid six that also came in the Hornet, while the 232 one barrel six was the only option. The Gremlin was thus hampered by the lack of a four-cylinder engine in a market segment where the competition was mostly fours, but that didn't hurt the Gremlin, at least not in the first few years. The American driver was just beginning to get acquainted with the subcompact car, and many of these drivers felt a bit uneasy about the perceived service life expectancy of a four-cylinder car. The Gremlin appealed to them as a reasonable compromise, and it was. Too, many American buyers were just stepping out of big and intermediate cars, so the smoothness, quietness and torque of the AMC six-cylinder engine was something they felt comfortable with. Later, when the subcompact market began to mature and a gas crisis hit, the lack of a four-cylinder engine would cause a great deal of soul searching, but now, in 1970, it was not a big issue.

One thing American Motors had not done in years was pioneer a new market segment, and it had to wrestle with its own insecurity when it came time to price the Gremlin. Because it was the only American subcompact on the market in 1970, it had no basis on which to figure a selling price. In the end, it was decided to offer a low bucks stripped car as a price leader at just $1879. This was for a car that was bare bones even for that market, with a plain bench front seat and no back seat at all, just rubber matted floor space. This was, in truth, very much a reemergence of the old Detroit practice of offering what it had called a business coupe, which all the lower-priced brands sold in the fifties and before. The business coupe, in Detroit parlance, had usually been a stripped two-door sedan with the back seat removed so that traveling salesmen could store samples in that area. How many had ever been sold is hard to say, but they were used more often as not as a way to advertise an extremely low price.

In the Gremlin's case, besides having no rear seat, the two-passenger model, as it was referred to, also had a fixed rear window so that storage area in the back could only be accessed from the doors. It didn't really matter, as AMC was smart enough to make a point of explaining that the lower-priced car held but two people, so hopefully no one felt deceived. Only 872 two-passenger Gremlins were built in 1970.

At any rate, the four-passenger Gremlin, at $1959, was still the lowest-priced American car on the market, save for the two-seater Gremlin. The four-seater was no luxury bucket, that was for certain, but did come with a fold-down rear seat, flip open rear tailgate window, and a much longer option list. Bucket seats, a big selling feature on imports in that decade, were optional, as were air conditioning, power steering and brakes, and many trim and appearance dress-up options.

The advertising played on the youthfulness of the car. Unlike Abernethy's campaigns, the new

Top: For 1970, the Rebel two-door hardtop received this new roofline. Bottom: The 1970 Rebel station wagon did not benefit from the sedan's restyling.

advertising hit home that this was a fun car that was practical instead of vice versa. The modern styling of the car was controversial among older people, which perhaps made it an even bigger hit with young people, but the crowds had seen a similar shape a few years before when the AMX GT concept car had been shown at all the major auto shows. It was at the very least seen as something that was on the leading edge, new, different, and that was where AMC wanted to be. Roy Chapin and Wells, Rich, Greene Inc. knew that it was going to take boldness and a bit of risk to revitalize the American Motors image. The image makeover had started three years before and it was working, but there was still a lot of damage left to be undone.

It could also be said that this was a further adjustment of image, for the AMC nameplate was now to be emphasized in advertising. The Rambler nameplate was eased out slowly, from 1965 to 1969, and an attempt to replace it with the AM trademark was started. The idea was that newsmen and the public would soon refer to the company as simply AM, much like General Motors is referred to as GM. That hadn't worked, maybe because enough time hadn't been allowed, but more likely just because it didn't slip off the tongue very easily. But a change had to be done, so it was decided now to concentrate on the AMC name. The new company logo, a stylized "A" done in red, white and blue, would now be used in conjunction with the words "American Motors" on all company press releases, letterheads, and literature.

For 1970, the Rebel's rear fenders were changed and the rear doors now had a pronounced "up-kick."

148

Limited edition 1970 Javelin, painted red, white and blue, featured the potent 390 cid V-8.

1970 Ambassador four-door sedan also received "up-kick" rear doors, although the lines were better balanced.

The balance of the AMC lineup for 1970 was carryover, as could be expected, for the cost of introducing the new Hornet sedans and the Gremlin was high. The midsize Rebel was back for another year, its last, it so happened. The Rebel hardtops got new rear quarter panels that gave them a lumpy, pregnant look and didn't really match well with the front end styling. One was left with the impression that two distinctly different cars had been welded together to make up one new car, and the truth was not too far removed from that. The four-door sedans got restyled rear doors that featured an upkick at the rear edge of the door upper. This again was an odd styling touch that did not enhance the cars at all; it instead made them look old-fashioned.

1970 Javelin SST.

1970 Javelin SST.

The Javelins were also back with no major changes. New sporty hoods were a welcome touch, and the revised grilles were very pleasing. The AMX had a mild face-lift of the hood/grille and was in its last year as a separate, distinct two-seat sports car. Not many were made for 1970, just 4116, but they carried a lot more image than the numbers would indicate. The Ambassador received the same new rear quarters as the Rebels, but they seemed a bit less offensive on the long wheelbase cars. Still, even the class and luxury of the Ambassador couldn't hide the fact that the new look for AMC's large and midsize hardtops was just not attractive.

The biggest news for American Motors came in February 1970, and it had nothing at all to do with cars. Roy Chapin had been looking at the Kaiser Jeep Corporation for many years and now decided to buy the company. It was a bold move, a gutsy move and the most controversial move of his career. AMC had been on the comeback trail for just a bit over two years and had managed in that time to make only meager profits, and that only by keeping a lock on the cash box. Chapin was spending a ton of money to buy Jeep. The purchase price came to $10 million in cash, $9,493,482 in serial notes, and 5,500,000 shares of AMC stock, for a total purchase price of $70,213,732. This was a pile of money in 1970, especially when it was being spent to buy a money-losing operation like Kaiser Jeep. Gerry Meyers, the manufacturing specialist Chapin had sent to look over Jeep's plants, felt that AMC had enough problems of its own and didn't need to go out and buy more. He was right in his way, that is, in the realm of his responsibilities and knowledge. But Roy Chapin knew a bit more about Kaiser Jeep and its potential. Remember Chapin had been in charge of AMC international sales for many years prior to his elevation to head all automotive activities. He had signed agreements with Kaiser Argentina to build Ramblers in the Kaiser plant there. Kaiser and AMC were partnered in manufacturing in Mexico as well. In both instances Chapin noticed how it was beneficial to have a truck builder and car builder teamed together, for the Mexican who owned a Jeep was likely to consider a Rambler when it came time to buy a car, as they were built under the same corporate roof.

American Motors had never offered trucks before. Its predecessor companies, both Nash and Hudson, had sold small numbers of trucks in the past, but the modern AMC never did. Chapin felt that offering the Jeep line would provide the synergies he had seen in the third world markets. Although Jeep was currently unprofitable, he knew that introducing AMC components into the Jeep line would help both lines by providing volume efficency they both needed. Chapin also wanted the experience and contacts of the Jeep people who sold products to the government, for that experience could help the company in future bidding for passenger car sales as well as Jeep vehicles.

But more than anything else, Chapin felt that the market for four-wheel-drive vehicles was going to explode in the seventies, and he wanted to make sure his company was there to profit from that growth. It was certainly difficult for the average person to discern any sort of full-scale movement coming in that part of the market. There were some sales to be made, no doubt about it, but an explosive market increase? It didn't seem likely to most people. One magazine ran a critical story about the purchase, dubbing it "Chapin's Folly." Chapin had to withstand some sharp critisism, but he did and the purchase of Kaiser Jeep went through.

It caused havoc with the financial reports for the year. In the annual report of 1970, a grim-looking Chapin had to report a loss for the year of $56.2 million. The buyout of Jeep had added a lot of dollar volume to the sales picture, as AMC net sales went to $1,089,787, the first time in years that the $1 billion mark was crossed. But there were also a lot of new employees, almost 6000 more, and that drove up the payroll to over a quarter of a billion dollars. Working capital dropped, never a good sign, to $76,239,000. This was a new American Motors that was birthing in 1970, and it wasn't a healthy child.

Chapin noted that the assimilation of Jeep was moving along, but was a major cause of the losses. Yet in his message to the stockholders he stated, "However -- and this we also want to emphasize -- Jeep can be and will be a major contributor to American Motors." That was hard to see, but it would certainly turn out to be true.

For the time being, it was decided to spin off the Jeep commercial and government vehicles into a separate General Products Division. Work was immediately begun to incorporate AMC engines and components into those Jeep vehicles that would be sold to the general public.

Sales of American Motors cars were off a bit in 1970, despite the new Gremlin and Hornet. Wholesale sales of 307,362 were noted worldwide, while Jeep vehicles came in at 93,171, also down from the prior year. Of that total, only about 30,000 Jeeps were retail units as the commercial products were the strong sellers. The combination of Jeep and AMC was about 400,000 units; not bad, but not very good either, and certainly not profitable. Chapin directed his marketing men to conduct research into the sport-utility vehicle market to find out what buyers now and in the near future would want in a four-wheel-drive vehicle, so that new models and trim packages could be developed to meet those customers' desires.

One extremely minor part of the purchase of Jeep was a prototype of what the Kaiser designers thought the future held for sport utilities. It was a low-slung two-passenger fiberglass-bodied four-wheel-drive sports car they called the Jeep XJ001. It was sharp, a real eye-catcher, and it came with a big AMC V-8 engine and full-time four-wheel-drive, but when AMC took over, they took a brief look and decided it was not going to ever be put into production. There were scant funds available to

Jeep XJ001, the prototype of a possible Jeep four-wheel drive sports car, was a true roadster, having no doors or top. It was shown in 1970.

AMX/3 in Rome. Although several were built and still exist, the AMX/3 was never put into regular production. AMC cancelled the program when costs got too high.

tool for redesigned core products and it was certain that this Jeep sports car could never sell in large volume. Still, frugal AMC never would let a perfectly good prototype go to waste, so the XJ001 was put to work at auto shows to draw attention to the AMC/Jeep exhibits.

Besides, AMC already had a sports car to show off. Teague and his team had been working on a dramatically styled two-seater that was not only the first American-designed mid-engine sports car, this one was actually planned for production. The AMX/3 was the latest and most developed in the long line of AMX show cars and was also the most dazzling. Designed by Teague, its chassis development was handed over to Bizzarini, a tuner and builder of exotic Gran Touring cars in Europe. Built in the small quantities planned, it would be a very expensive sports car, but was almost certain to run that other American sports car, Corvette, into the weeds.

1970 Rebel "Machine," a.k.a. "The Flying Brick."

It would also be a much more shapely package than this year's attempt at building a hot rod. The 1970 Rebel Machine had garnered a fair run of press coverage. With its 340 horsepower 390 cid engine, it sure had the muscle needed to move its 3,650 pound weight, and the factory paint schemes of red and blue stripes on a white backround recalled the flashy SC/Rambler of 1969 without duplicating it. It was an attractive package that found over 2300 buyers, but it was not the exotic continental car that the AMX/3 was, not by any stretch of the imagination. Still, with the Rebel Machine, AMX, and the Javelin, AMC had certainly made an impression on the youth of the country.

But 1970 ended on a sour note because, despite the AMX that was being developed, despite the

If you had to compete with GM, Ford and Chrysler, what would you do?

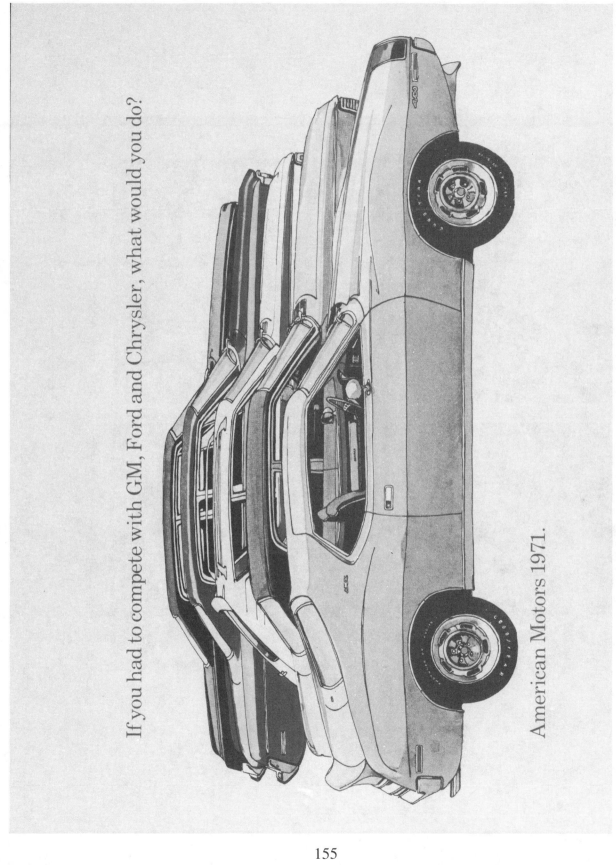

American Motors 1971.

For 1971, AMC appealed to armchair quarterbacks everywhere when it asked, "If you had to compete with GM, Ford and Chrysler, what would you do?"

The Matador was designed to make the other intermediates look stingy.

It has more room for you and your family than any other car in its class.

To make the ride even more comfortable, we built it on a longer wheelbase than you get with Torino, Satellite and Chevelle.

As you can see, when we redesign a car, as we did with the Rebel, (so much so that we changed its name) we don't merely glamorize it.

In times like these, we thought extra room for no extra money would be appreciated.

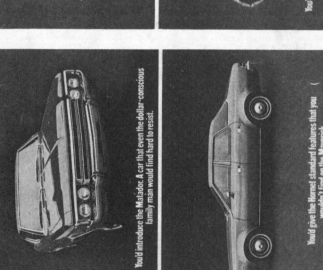

You'd introduce the Matador. A car that even the dollar-conscious family man would find hard to resist.

The Hornet, dedicated to the proposition that little doesn't have to mean cheap, gives you a standard engine that's 62 cubic inches bigger and 35 horsepower stronger than the Maverick's.

Our two-door generously makes room for one more passenger than theirs.

And when it comes down to details, we give you a step-on parking brake, a counterbalanced hood and a glove box.

Whereas they give you a pull handle brake, a prop-up hood and no glove box.

Yet the list price of the two cars is virtually the same.

It would appear that the Hornet is the better buy.

You'd give the Hornet standard features that you wouldn't find on the Maverick.

The Sportabout will make the American housewife feel more like a woman and less like a teamster.

It's styled along the lines of a sports car instead of a station wagon.

And with a turning circle identical to VW's, it's easy to handle.

Now ladies, you can park without the danger of developing your biceps.

And let's face it girls, the 58.3 cubic feet of load space is plenty for most of the things you do.

So you can see why we like to think of the Sportabout as our little contribution to Woman's Liberation.

You'd design the Sportabout. A car that could do more for the American housewife than all the haircoloring, lip gloss and false eyelashes put together.

The Gremlin, in addition to its trend-setting proclivities, beats the competition to the punch another way.

By being more fun to drive.

The chief reason for this is that the Gremlin comes with a 6 cylinder engine as standard equipment.

Instead of the 4 that the other subcompacts give you.

The maneuverability of the Gremlin is another contributor to the fun.

Its turning circle, at 33 feet, is 3 feet less than Volkswagen's.

So, if you're going to buy an American made subcompact, buy the original.

You'd start a small car revolution by coming out with America's first subcompact: the Gremlin.

The new Javelin may not be quite as lovable as the old Javelin, but it's a lot tougher.

We made it longer, wider and lower to make it ride better.

And to make it look better while it's riding better, we sculptured the hood into a fast, glacial slope. and we raised the fenders around the tires.

If that isn't enough for you to intimidate friends and or competitors, we're offering a range of engines up to a 401 CID 4-barrel V-8.

We may lose a few dollars out for customers, but as I think we'll gain a few purists.

You'd make the Javelin the hairiest looking sporty car in America, even at the risk of scaring some people off.

The Ambassador is a *legitimate* luxury car. Not by mere decree, but because it's got the goods.

Nonetheless, its price is competitive with Galaxie, Impala and Fury.

We could go on with details about coil spring seats, upholstery, etc., but why embroider a very clear proposition.

At American Motors, luxury isn't something we just talk about, it's a value that we express in tangible terms.

You'd make the Ambassador the only car line in America with both air-conditioning and automatic transmission as standard equipment. ▼◀ **American Motors**

If you had to compete with GM, Ford and Chrysler

To locate your nearest American Motors dealer or to get your copy of the new 1971 American Motors

what would you do?

catalog, call, no charge (800) 243-6000 any time, any day. In Connecticut (800) 942-0655.

1971 advertising campaign asked the question and provided the answer.

new Hornet and new Gremlin, even despite the whole new division that had been purchased, in the end the company had generated a loss, and a rather large one at that. The stockholders and financiers for the most part would be patient, for this fellow Chapin had shown them he had the gumption to make the hard choices when he had to. Chapin had at the very least flown the company out its 1967 tailspin, and at least he seemed to be trying to rebuild the company into something worthwhile now. Their patience would not be endless, Chapin knew that, and 1971 had to be a better year or there would be hell to pay.

For 1971 a new advertising slogan was developed, one that would go down in history as the slogan that changed AMC. For 1971, American Motors Corporation asked a simple yet profound question: "If you had to compete with GM, Ford and Chrysler, what would you do?" The brochures and the TV ads provided the answer, which was actually a separate answer for each car line. "You'd bring out the first American subcompact, the Gremlin, six months before GM and Ford." "You'd bring out the Hornet Sportabout, the only compact wagon on the market." Each line had an answer to the basic question which stressed its advantages over the competition and provided additional copy to further explain. What this advertising campaign really provided, besides a focal point for the basic product message, was a rallying cry for the public to join forces with the little guy and root for the underdog. It has been said that we Americans hate a loser and love a winner, and that may or may

The hottest-selling Hornet for 1971 was the new Sportabout wagon, with styling that was hinted at by the AMX III prototype.

not be true. But what is certainly true, has always been true, and will probably remain true is that Americans love it when the little guy wins. The underlying theme to the "Rocky" series of movies is that of the struggling unknown who makes it to the top, becomes a hero, is the champ, by trying harder and fighting fair. And with the work of a forgotten copywriter, that image was instantly transferred to American Motors, driving out the last vestige of loser and endowing it with the gutsy underdog image it would use to make its run for the big time. AMC was no longer a goat. AMC was now a contender.

Hornet sedan for 1971.

The 1971 line was a very good group of cars. The big product news was the Sportabout, a four-door station wagon version of the Hornet. The Sportabout carried the styling theme first shown in 1967 on an AMX concept car called AMX III. (The AMX/3 and AMX III were completely different cars, as were the AMX/2 and AMX II.) Sportabout had a fastback styled roofline and a hatch rear opening instead of the traditional station wagon tailgate. This was to make the Sportabout feel less like a station wagon and more like a sport sedan, and it did prove to be very popular. The Hornet sedans were improved by the addition of the 232 cid six as standard equipment on all models, and the addition of a new model, the SC/360. The SC/360 Hornet was an attempt to recapture some of the magic and sales success of the old SC/Rambler of 1969. Equipped with a 360 cid two barrel V-8 and trimmed with styled wheels and side stripes, the SC/360 offered high performance at low dollars, just $2663 base price.

The Gremlin really began to come on strong in 1971. The two-seater remained in the lineup, now

Gremlin for 1971 got the new 232 cid engine as standard with the 258 cid as an option. The roof rack was a popular option.

priced at $1899 base, while the four-seater took a bigger price hike to $1999, still a buck under that $2000 mark and under the $2090 price of the new Chevy Vega. The new Ford Pinto came in under the Gremlin's price, at $1,949 for a stripped four-seater, a significant advantage in the low-price market, but, of course, the Gremlin two-passenger model was still the lowest-priced car made in America. It was not much of an advantage, though, as the two-seater was not a volume model. Still, the lowest cost title was still AMC's, at least for now.

Gremlin received the 232 cid engine as standard equipment, just like the Hornet, as the 199 engine went out of production. Sport wheel covers, fat tires, and new colors were new enhancements. A new trim package was introduced that really started sales going, the "X" package. The Gremlin "X" had custom bucket seats, carpeting, slot style wheels, fat D70-14 tires, cute side stripes, and a painted grille. A painted rear panel carried a decal that showed the engine size in liters, i.e., 3.8 for the 232 cid six. The X package transformed the economy look to a sporty look with one simple tick of the option list and sold in incredible numbers. The company accountants were pleased as the trim packages carried a high profit margin while the marketing men loved having a small car that sold on looks rather than price alone. The 258 cid six-cylinder engine, a longer stroke version of the 232,

Early in the 1971 model year, the 40,000th Gremlin was built, highlighted here by Terri Shepard, a secretary at American Motors.

was now available as an option. Still being used, however, were two engineering holdouts, the three-speed manual transmission that still had a non-synchromesh first gear, and vacuum-powered windshield wipers, two features that just about every other car company had long since dropped. It tarnished the modern image of AMC to have these stale items on its cars, but costs were very closely watched and changes would have to wait for now.

Besides, there was so much other new product to look at. The one the reporters ran to was the all-new Javelin. Javelin was much larger for 1971, broad-shouldered and long with a distinctly heavy look that seemed a clone of the Mustang, only with more surface detailing and better stance. The AMX now shared the same wheelbase and body with the Javelin and was referred to as the Javelin/AMX, so the two-seater was gone and gone for good. This was taken by some as foreshadowing the introduction of the AMX/3 sportscar, but it didn't happen that way.

This new Javelin series rode a 110-inch wheelbase, one inch longer than the original Javelin, and was a whopping 3.3 inches wider as well, not causing much of a weight increase, but causing the car

160

to look much heavier, less of a sprinter. This can accurately be called a mistake by the AMC product planners, and by Dick Teague himself, for the new Javelin did not sell as well as the old Javelin despite the very large investment in design and tooling for the car. The AMX, of course, cost less to tool for as the only unique pieces were the grille and some trim. Yet, even the new four-seat AMX sold fewer than the old model. This lack of sales success hurt the bottom line several ways. Lack of volume meant lack of profit for that car line, but it also meant that the dollars spent on the new Jave-

Exaggerated fender bulges and a deeply recessed grille were hallmarks of the all-new Javelin for 1971.

lin would not be available for putting some other, potentially profitable new car into production. Other product programs would have to be cut or stretched to make up for the failure of the Javelin/AMX.

It wasn't that the new car looked bad. On the contrary, it was handsome, better looking than the Dodge and Plymouth pony cars, even better looking than the renowned Mustang. It was just that the whole new generation of pony cars was larger, heavier, more expensive and less responsive than before, and were being pushed with much larger motors that made them much quicker, but also

The all new AMX for 1971 was now a performance model in the Javelin line. It no longer had a unique body/chassis.

The twin-canopy sculptured roof was a strong styling touch on the 1971 Javelin.

162

For 1971, the front end of the Rebel wagon received a pleasing reedesign, and the name was changed to Matador.

much more expensive to purchase and to insure. It was all a case of too much, and the public wasn't buying it in anywhere near the volume of previous years. The market loss cost Ford, GM and Chrysler some profits, no doubt, but they had numerous other lines of cars that sold in the hundreds of thousands, and could cover their losses. American Motors' volume wasn't great in any segments, really, and it could not afford a profit loss of any size.

In the intermediate market there was a new AMC entry that looked familiar: the new Matador, AMC's competition for Chevelle, Torino and Plymouth Satellite, was heavily based on the Rebel, which it replaced. Built on a longer 118-inch wheelbase, the front end was all new, with a smoother fender shape and a softer grille appearance. The overall frontal appearance was very handsome with a suggestion of Plymouth, but better. Considering that this was a face-lift, it was a remarkable job. Not so with the rest of the car, for the lumpy quarter panels with the odd rear wheel openings, and the rear door shape of the 1970 Rebel marred the style. The restyling of the back half of the 1970 Rebel had been done just so the new front end of the 1971 intermediate would blend in, creating a new car. The longer wheelbase helped cure the stubby front look of the Rebel, and if the rear fenders had been restyled, it could have been a sharp car. As it was, the sales pitch for the Matador was value for the model range had no stripped-down price leaders; every Matador was well trimmed. A hardtop coupe, four-door sedan and station wagon were in the lineup.

The Ambassador range was a carryover with a more classic grille that was a beauty and some trim and option changes. The sedan was getting more and more handsome each year, while the coupe suffered along with the rear fenders and bizarre roofline of the Matador.

Of course, for 1971 AMC had to fine-tune the Jeep vehicles. The CJ-5 and CJ-6 were the Jeeps most people remembered, but the Jeep Wagoneer and the Gladiator trucks had a great deal of profit potential. The Jeep Commando was somewhere in between the size of a CJ and a Wagoneer, and that might be an area of future growth, but for now, engineering worked on incorporating as many AMC components as possible into the Jeep line. It was easier than some people thought, as the Wagoneer/ Gladiator had been using AMC engines already, although not exclusively. Where the trouble came in was the CJ/Commando vehicles, which shared the same basic chassis and used the Jeep four-cylinder and V-8 engines. The Jeep four was a rough, underpowered motor that dated back to the forties and was past its prime, while the V-6 was more modern. The V-6 had been developed by Buick in the early sixties for use in its compact cars. The tooling had been sold to Jeep when a lack of volume made it uneconomical for Buick to continue to offer it.

AMC's engineering team, led by Marvin Stuckey, felt that the AMC 232 cid six was both smoother and longer lived, due to its low stress seven main bearing design, than the Jeep V-6, and it was cheaper to build the 232, it being a volume product. So changes were made to allow the use of the AMC sixes in the CJ series, as well as the AMC V-8. They would be ready for the 1972 models.

Handsome and distinctive, the Ambassador's front end styling is in sharp contrast to the roof and rear wheel openings as shown on this 1971 model.

164

Several limited run specialty models were added to the Jeep line, including a high-performance Hurst/Jeepster Commando and a limited-run Renegade model of the CJ-5. The Hurst/Jeepster didn't attract many shoppers, but the Renegade proved more popular than expected. Both models were basically sport trim and bigger engines.

The 1972 Gremlin, which had a V-8 option, was very popular with young people.

The AMC manufacturing team began to retool the CJ body, which was a simple design made complicated by the use of smaller stampings that had to be welded into bigger sections before being assembled on the chassis. Additionally, AMC streamlined the assembly line, installing more modern procedures and better tools. In the case of the CJ, it was decided to continue with the same styling despite the retooling, as the look itself was cherished by the public. The advantage AMC got from the retooling was in the increased productivity of the rejuvenated assembly line.

American Motors also began to merge what Meyers called "Jeep's ragtag distribution system" with the AMC network, signing up many AMC dealers to add the Jeep to their showroom. In truth, this alone might have turned Jeep around, for by 1970, it had a small, very weak dealer body. The average AMC dealer was a much better businessman than the average Jeep dealer and could provide the marketing representation the Jeep deserved.

The General Products Division was reorganized as a wholly owned subsidiary, AM General, in charge of production and sales of military and postal vehicles.

For 1971, the pieces of the puzzle were all at hand, and the picture of the future was beginning to take shape. But 1971 was yet another year of working towards the future; it was not the future itself. Domestic wholesale sales of passenger car and Jeeps came in at 286,597 units, and overseas sales were 58,128 units. This sounded worse than it was, as the figures no longer included military or postal vehicle sales. AMC netted a profit for the year of $10,177,000 on sales of $1,232,558,000, which was a lot of dollar volume if not a lot of profit. Chapin pointed out that it represented a strong turnaround from the high loss of 1970, but the stockholders were getting a bit tired of all this annual talk about the bright future AMC had. What it wanted now was a few years of solid profits with no excuses.

Things actually were better than they looked, for the profit had come despite a run of new product introductions that had been expensive. The Hornet, Gremlin, Matador and Javelin/AMX were all new cars introduced in just a two-year period. The Matador didn't sell very well, but it had potential. The Hornet sedans had sold poorly as the emphasis was put on the new Sportabout. But Hornet was a contender and volume could be built on the foundation it had started. The Gremlin had real potential, as it was perhaps the most recognizable car on the road and was fast earning a solid reputation. With careful marketing, Gremlin could sell in the kind of volume Chapin only dreamed about. For 1972, it was up to the marketing people to exploit the product advantages AMC now had.

Still selling strong, the 1972 Hornet Sportabout.

What AMC Vice President Gerry Meyers wanted to do for 1972 was address the issue of product quality in a way that had not been done at AMC since Romney left, that is, continuous improvement of the basic product, adding more value each year and achieving higher quality than the competition. For 1972, Meyers formed a task force that generated 102 engineering improvements in the AMC car lines, aimed at improving the car and reducing warranty claims.

First thing to go was the old Borg-Warner automatic transmission, replaced by a Chrysler-built unit that shifted smoother, was quieter and didn't need periodic adjustments or oil changes. Door hardware was improved, radios were improved, and new quality standards were written that sharply reduced the failure rate that would be tolerated on parts received at the factory. These improvements

166

The Hornet "X" package for 1972 was an attempt to increase sales the way the "X" package spurred Gremlin sales. The Hornet "X" failed to attract many sales, however.

167

were explained in detail to the press, who hailed them as a sign of a change in the way automakers ran their businesses, at least one automaker. Robert Lund, Detroit editor for *Popular Mechanics* magazine, summed it up in one oft-repeated paragraph. "The best cars out of Detroit this year," he wrote, "in terms of the way they're put together may come out of Wisconsin. That's where American Motors makes 'em." The model range was tightened, dropping from 21 models in 1971 to just 15 models in 1972. All the lowest line cars were dropped. "No more strippies," according to Garry Meyers. " We're going bottomless for 1972." Important changes also included the addition of electric windshield wipers and washers, finally doing away with the old-fashioned vacuum type. The engineering improvements were mostly under the skin, but exterior changes did appear as well. Javelin got a new, much better looking grille as well as new stripes as an option. Gremlin got nicer interior trim and improved bucket seats. A powerful new option on the Gremlin was the 304 cid V-8 engine, a drop-in fit since it was already offered on the Hornet. The auto press went in a big way for the idea of a low-cost subcompact car with a V-8 engine and loved the performance, if not the looks, of the Gremlin. One magazine called it "the poor man's Corvette." The stripped two-passenger model was not offered; it was dropped in an attempt to simplify the AMC assembly line, and anyway, it never sold well. The Gremlin now started at $1,999 for a six-cylinder four-passenger sedan, same as the 1971 model had, an excellent value especially when the new quality improvements were considered.

Hornet had many changes, chief of which was the dropping of the stripped base series. All 1972 Hornets were SSTs but were only a few dollars more expensive than the base cars had been. The 1972 Hornet SST two-door, for example, was just $3 more, $2177, than the 1971 base sedan, yet came with rear seat arm rests and ashtray, a cigarette lighter, full carpeting throughout the interior, locking glovebox, under dash package tray, and custom steering wheel, all of which the 1971 model did not have. It was an excellent value and a smart way to market the product.

1972 Matador station wagon had curious wood trim.

The Hornet SC/360 was not offered for 1972, although the reason why it was dropped was just because it had bombed on the market. The low price didn't attract any buyers, even though the performance was very good and could be further pumped up with optional equipment. AMC had not found whatever magic had worked on the SC/Rambler, as the Hornet SC sold just 784 units, a truly dismal showing. Since the engineering work to fit the 360 engine in the Hornet had already been done, the 360 two-barrel engine was offered optionally on the 1972 Hornet. Several appearance packages were added to the Hornet option list, including a Hornet X package, but they never caught on or sold like the Gremlin X did.

A more interesting package was the Hornet Rallye, which came with bucket seats, front disc brakes, handling package, quick-ratio manual steering, full synchromesh three-speed transmission with floor shift, and a sports steering wheel. The Rallye was equipped for "go" and not for show, like the Hornet X package, but failed to interest many buyers despite its unique and purposeful standard equipment.

Matadors and Ambassadors got detail changes, as the emphasis began to be directed even further on the small car lines. All AMC products received one feature that set them apart and above the rest of the car market. For 1972, AMC introduced a completely revised and enhanced new car warranty, along with a program of ensuring that new car customers would be satisfied with their AMC car. Called the "Buyer Protection Plan," this warranty/guarantee program was heavily advertised by AMC in a series of television ads and a strong print campaign that explained the Buyer Protection Plan. The ads were used to highlight the Buyer Protection Plan, explaining that it consisted of: 1) a strong guarantee in plain English; 2) a more thoroughly checked car from the factory to the dealer; 3) a loaner car when you need it; and 4) a direct line to Detroit, toll free.

For 1972, the Matador received a revised grille.

169

Jeep J-4000 pickup for 1972 was tough and dependable.

The Buyer Protection Plan was in direct response to research AMC had conducted that indicated a high level of dissatisfaction among new car buyers of all makes, especially with regard to product defects and the hassle of having to return to the dealer to have the defects repaired. The imports were feeding on this growing angst, and it was a perfect objection for AMC to focus on. Gerry Meyers' campaign to drastically improve AMC's quality had been aimed at helping the program by ensuring the factory could deliver the quality that the Buyer Protection Plan implied. As it happened, AMC's product quality was dramatically better than in some recent years. In certain areas, AMC was seen as better than the Big Three makes, in areas like paint work and engine longevity. The AMC seven main bearing engine was generally recognized as one of the best and sturdiest on the market, perhaps the very best. The AMC dealer body, for the most part, helped out by performing a more conscientious predelivery servicing and by road-testing to wring out any squeaks and rattles that may have been overlooked. AMC backed its promises by being more liberal in paying warranty claims so dealers would perform warranty work without fear of being stuck for the bill. Chapin acknowledged that the more free-spending attitude regarding warranty costs was expensive, but he knew it was vital to the success of the Buyer Protection Plan.

And successful it was. The Buyer Protection Plan was one of the most talked about new features of the 1972 auto market. AMC was awarded high recognition for its pro-consumer stance, and the buying public fell in love with the whole idea. The American motorist was, by this time, getting more than just a little bit tired of the sloppy workmanship that had gradually been creeping into the cars they were buying. They felt cheated by it and humiliated by the poor service they received at many domestic dealers. Some revolted by buying imports, and here the Japanese were harvesting new customers. Many others revolted by going shopping, for the first time ever, at their local AMC dealers.

170

The Jeep Commando received a new front end design and AMC engines, including the 304 cid V-8 for 1972.

It all moved the needle in the right direction as the company recorded domestic passenger car sales of 303,000, the best in seven years, and domestic sales of Jeep vehicles of 46,000 units. In the international markets, a total of 59,251 units were sold, a slight increase as well. Unit sales of military trucks were no longer reported, as these were counted as part of a newly retitled government products division formerly called General Products and now called AM General. AM General results were only noted in dollar amounts, such as total sales, and order backlogs.

Jeep CJ-5 for 1972 now offered the AMC 304 cid V-8 as an option. Power steering and power brakes were new options.

The 408,000 AMC and Jeep worldwide wholesale sales figures were a sharp improvement. More importantly, these sales results were profitable, as AMC turned in a net profit for 1972 of $30,157,000, nearly triple from the prior year. Working capital recovered, now totaling $148,399,000, a hefty sum indeed. Total sales volume for the year set a new record, $1.4 billion, almost twice the amount of just three years before. The net earnings figure was the best since 1964, although the 1964 results reflected pure profit from operations, while the 1972 results included a loss carryforward of $13.7 million. Inflation was heating up, so the results also reflected inflated dollars, but all in all, it was a decent year.

Roy Chapin gazed into his crystal ball, thought he saw the future, and reported it to his fellow shareholders. The game plan was to continue to build on the momentum they now had while searching for niches in the market where the consumer was not being adequately served. AMC explained it as its new "Philosophy of Difference," which meant that it had to offer the consumer something different from the Big Three and the imports to win new business. As the annual report explained, "It means doing things differently and distinctively -- with the willingness to assume the risks of innovation." But did they really understand the risks of innovation? Was AMC really ready to assume those risks?

Chapin also noted that the goal for the later part of the decade was to increase combined Jeep/AMC sales to the 600,000 range, bold for a worldwide goal, but he was talking 600,000 units just in the United States. The outlook for 1973 was bright, the brightest it had been in years. The Gremlin line would do well, a new Hornet model was being added to the line, the Jeep line would show many improvements, and the market itself was expected to improve. The auto press was in love with AMC again, no longer writing page after page of doom and gloom articles about its struggles. Roy Chapin also began a diversification program to try to lessen the effects of the cyclical nature of the auto business. New subsidiaries were AM Data Systems, American Motors Leasing Corporation, and Coleman Products Company, a maker of wire harnesses. Added to the two small plastics companies already part of AMC, Evart Products and Winsor Plastics, the plan was beginning to look like something. The Canadian company that cast the blocks for AMC engines had already been added to the corporate directory; Holmes Foundry, Ltd. was its name, and it was a good, solid company.

The big news in diversification was that AM General was going to enter the transit bus field. Mass transit was a hot topic in the early seventies, a response to the problems of air pollution and overcrowded highways. It was noted that a substantial part of the American fleet of transit, or city use, buses was old and in need of replacement. It was hoped, indeed expected, that the combination of the need to replace many of the existing buses and the need for more buses would be enough of a market to satisfy the two existing bus builders, General Motors and Flxible, while providing room for a plucky newcomer like AMC. Chapin's designers were working hard on their new bus designs, integrating many new features to make certain that they won a fair share of the market.

Thus, a confident American Motors began yet another year in the car business. Confidence was justified, for the 1973 line of AMC cars was the best in years. Bright new colors dominated the lots as purples, yellows, bronzes, and greens appeared. The newest member of the Hornet family was the

The 1973 Hornet hatchback: Stylish and practical, it was a hit.

173

"The styling coup of '73"

When we introduced the Hornet Hatchback this fall, Car & Driver Magazine called it "The styling coup of '73."

And along with sportscar styling, you get room to travel in; 23 cubic feet of cargo space with the back seat folded down.

Now we've added something else. An optional Levi's interior. The look of jeans, copper buttons, orange stitching...even a Levi's tab.

So if you want the style, the performance, the room, the Levi's interior and the American Motors Buyer Protection Plan, get a Hornet Hatchback at your AMC dealer, where he'll give you a good deal and a good deal more.

Buckle up for safety.

AMC ▅▐ Hornet
We back them better because we build them better.   63

*AMC made good use of the **Car and Driver** quote.*

A new idea: Hatchbacks were still uncommon in 1973, and the Hornet was the best looking of them all.

Hornet hatchback. The hatchback was a new concept to most Americans, foreign and exciting, practical and perky all at once. Other makes were showing hatchbacks this year, but the Hornet hatchback was the best-looking of the bunch, not a cut up two-door sedan, but clearly a new model in the lineup using its own roofline, rear fenders and hatch. *Car and Driver* magazine called it "the styling coup of 1973," a quote that AMC played up in its print advertising.

The Buyer Protection Plan was still featured on the first pages of the sales catalogs, it being a good selling point. Gremlin received still more improvements and refinements. The non-synchromesh transmission was replaced by a full synchro three-speed that now came with a floor shifter as standard equipment. The cheap 13-inch wheels and tires of prior years were upgraded to 6.45 x 14, still a skinny tread but better. Stripes and trims were revised a bit. The big news on the interior was a new option, Levi's blue denim trim for the bucket seats and door panels. Since Levi's blue jeans were the uniform of the day for hip young people, that image became a part of the Gremlin image. The Levi's trim was a very well received product innovation, and AMC was acclaimed for it.

In the Hornet line, the SST designation was dropped as all models were now just Hornet. Changes were few on the sedans. The new three-speed full synchromesh transmission was standard, while the X and Rallye packages were no longer available. The X package was still offered on the Sportabout, but it was expected to be most popular on the new hatchback. The Sportabout got a new interior trim package designed by noted fashion designer Aldo Gucci. The "Gucci Sportabout," as it was called, carried seat covers and door panels that wore Gucci's trademark green and red stripes on a beige backround. Sportabouts additionally could be had with upscale trim as on the Sportabout D/L. This package was most complete, including woodgrain panels on the outside of the doors, roof rack with air deflector, and individual reclining seats in plush "Scorpio" cloth. The packages were part of a try

175

at moving the average Hornet buyer a bit up the price ladder to where better profits could be made, while enhancing the image of the AMC product.

Javelin and AMX were carryover again, and not much was new on them. By now it was clear to AMC that the ponycar market was dead and that they would never get back their investment in the Javelin/AMX. The cars were in the line simply to provide a full lineup and a few extra sales, and anyway, the press corps liked to hotrod them at new car time. To continue the overall theme of fashion interiors, Javelin was offered with a new interior of bold red and white stripes applied symmetrically to the seats and carried over to the headliner as well. The effect was startling to say the least. Fashion designer Pierre Cardin designed the interior of the "Cardin Javelin," as it was called. A limited run was made of a special "Trans-Am Victory" Javelin to celebrate the victory of the George Follmer and Roy Woods in the Trans-Am racing series. The T/A Javelins came with E70x14 white letter tires mounted on slotted wheels and a fender decal, all at no extra charge.

Matadors came with a slightly redesigned grille, new colors and a few other changes, but for the

Denim clad model shows off the Levi's Gremlin for 1973. Note the revised "X" striping and Levi's decal.

176

Dick Teague restyled the Hornet front end into a softer, sedate look for 1973.

most part they were again carryover cars. The Ambassador line received similar small changes, but for 1973, the base line SST series was dropped, and the emphasis was on more and greater luxury, as the Brougham models were the only ones offered. The Ambassador had a great reputation as a solid luxury class car, but the styling was beginning to get stale, and some magazines began to speculate when a new Ambassador/Matador line would debut.

Prices were up for 1973, now starting at $2098 for Gremlin and $2298 for the Hornet two-door sedan. The new hatchback came in at $2449, a better profit maker since it cost about the same to build as the sedan. The top of the line, the Ambassador Brougham station wagon, was $4861.

Jeeps received many changes in 1973. The J series trucks got new double-walled pickup boxes with tailgates that now opened with one hand. Dashboards were upgraded as well. The big product news was an all-new type of four-wheel-drive system. Called "Quadra Trac," this new system was a full-time four-wheel-drive based on the Fergusson "master differential" concept. The system utilized a third, centralized differential that provided the torque relief neccessary to allow driving on hard, dry surfaces. It worked automatically and quietly, unnoticed by the average driver, but the benefits it provided were the elimination of locking hubs on the wheels, the end of having to get out of the vehicle to engage or disengage the front axle, and the elimination of the "mystery" of four-wheel-

American Motors featured optional design interiors for 1973. Top left: Levi's denim option for the Gremlin and Hornet hatchback. Top right: Gucci interior for the Sportabout. Bottom left: Domino print for the Hornet hatchback and AMX. Bottom right: Cardin's Javelin interior.

1973 Javelin had a new grille and smooth roof design. Background: 1973 AMX.

179

drive systems. Quadra Trac also offered greatly improved traction, along with the ability to drive on any sort of surface, good or bad, without having to use a lever to switch in and out of four-wheel-drive. It cost a modest amount as an option but did cause fuel economy to suffer a bit.

Quadra Trac was offered that first year on Jeep J series pickups and on the Wagoneer, Jeep's full-size four-door station wagon. These two lines made up what became known as the senior line of Jeeps, with the CJ and Commando being the junior line.

Jeep's CJ also got an improved dash design, and in January 1973, the Renegade package became a regular option. The package consisted of performance and appearance items, such as 304 V-8 engine, sporty wheels with H78 x 15 tires, wheel lip extensions, hood stripes and bucket seats. The Commando line received a minor upgrading only as it was getting a bit stale and was due to be replaced by a new model.

Whether it was the good price/value relationship, the innovative interiors, the bold colors, or the sporty packages that did it is difficult to ascertain, but the net effect was an increase in car sales, a nice increase of 25 percent to 380,000 domestic sales. AMC's share of the U.S. market rose as well, to 3.8 percent, up from 3.3 percent the year before. Jeep vehicle sales were up sharply as well, to 67,000 units domestically. To add another layer of good news, even international sales were up, to a total of 67,374 Jeep and AMC vehicles, with the big gains coming from Canadian and Latin American markets. This added up to a total of over 514,000 units.

The Matador for 1973 came with a very slightly revised grille.

The 1973 Ambassador had one of the longest standard equipment lists in the industry, including air conditioning, automatic transmission, V-8 engine, power steering, power disc brakes, radio, tinted glass and whitewall tires.

Total dollar sales were an astounding $1,739,025, up more than a billion dollars from just four years earlier, up $335,222,000 from 1972. Earnings required a bit of an explanation, as earnings from operations were $75,626,000 before taxes, $44,526,000 after taxes. A tax loss carryforward and deferred tax benefit of $41,450,000 combined to make the net profit for the year $85,976,000.

Hornet retail sales ended up at over 120,000 units. Sales of the new Hornet hatchback were particularly gratifying, as were sales of the Sportabout, still the only American compact station wagon on the market. Gremlin retail sales were over 115,000 units. The rest of the line sold in lesser numbers, as AMC was clearly attracting the small car crowd.

American Motors turned in an excellent year and was afforded the accolades of the business community, Wall Street, and the press. Few were bold enough or reckless enough to point out the few weak spots in American Motors. The benefit of hindsight allows the writer to do just that, look back and see where things began to go wrong, and the first inklings appeared at the end of 1973.

First, American Motors was selling high volume only in the less profitable compact and subcompact markets. While these markets were vital to the success of AMC, they did not attract the higher profits available just a notch up the ladder in the intermediate segment. When George Romney had

Wagons ho! The 1973 AMC line-up included station wagons in the Ambassador, Matador and Hornet lines.

first set AMC on the road to success, he had done it by offering the 1956 Rambler, a car just one size down from the full-size car so common to Americans. Although the 1956 Rambler's wheelbase of 108 inches matched the wheelbase of the newer Hornet, the Hornet was in the small end of the market and was roughly comparable to the old Rambler American, a low-price, low-margin car, what Romney used to call the second car in a two-car family. The Gremlin was cut from similar cloth in that it appealed to young people buying their first car or older people buying a solid, inexpensive second car.

None of this was bad, and Chapin must be commended for getting people to buy *any* type of AMC car again. The problem was that the traditional, high margin business that AMC needed to get back into was the intermediate segment, where it now fielded the dowdy Matador as its entry. The Matador was, after all, a very thinly disguised Rebel, and most of the newer bodywork it now carried was unfortunate looking. The automotive press was being nice when it reported on the Matador, reporting its solid construction, excellent room and ride, and the good overall value it represented. But it wasn't too many more years before this same press turned, like the little boy in the crowd who hollered about the emperor's new clothes, and informed the public that the Matador was an ugly car.

The Matador was a good car, and it shared its body with the Ambassador, so its cost effectiveness was good, too. The problem was that while the Matador/Ambassador generated enough volume to be profitable, they did not generate enough volume to pay for the complete redesign they so badly needed. The new car market was going to continue to turn, slowly at times, away from the domestic standard full-sized car, as gas shortages, inflated car prices and smaller families all tipped the market in favor of smaller cars. But those people moving out of full-sized cars were not going to move directly into a Gremlin. No, they would move down a notch or two to the intermediate class car. Ford recognized this and was hard at work designing a radically different car to meet this new demand.

The Hornet chassis that Dick Teague designed was a touch of pure genius, a design that was inexpensive to build yet one that allowed several body types and models to be derived from it: the Hornet sedans, the Sportabout, the hatchback and the Gremlin. The small pickup truck that was to have been a part of the line, the Cowboy, was nixed by management when demand for the regular Hornets exceeded projections. In the styling studio, clay models were being worked on to create a sporty car based on the Gremlin, a car that might be put into production. It was a very successful platform in the spirit of Romney's old shared chassis program.

What was needed now was a second platform to replace the existing Ambassador/Matador platform. This new platform could use some of the tricks of component sharing learned in the Hornet program and should be planned for high volume, spinning off two- and four-door sedans and a station wagon, the sorts of models most desired in that size car. By rights it should be smaller than the current Matador, which was really oversized for the way the market was moving, and it should use fewer styling tricks than the old car, for those sorts of things go out of style too soon, leaving the company with an old-fashioned car.

The more upright styling of the European sedans was just coming into vogue in America; the "Mercedes look." Wasn't that what George Romney said was the idea behind the 1963 Rambler? It was, and it was still a good idea for a small maker like AMC. By utilizing the four square solid style of the Mercedes sedan, AMC would be able to keep the car on the market longer than usual, again to reduce its tooling costs and allow the higher margin it needed to survive and prosper. Ideally, the new Matador and Ambassador should share the same wheelbase as well as body, to effect the greatest savings. Differentiation could be achieved as it had been in 1963, by the Matador being offered as the six-cylinder sedan while the Ambassador would be an eight-cylinder car. The auto press would love it and write more glowing reports of the clever way that AMC was competing in the market and the great way it was offering new value in a mid-size car. Later on, the Javelin/AMX could be redesigned on the Hornet chassis to complete the transition to a low-cost/high-volume manufacturer. It was all there for the taking, but nobody realized it.

In his annual report to stockholders, Roy Chapin mentioned that substantial expenditures would be required to maintain AMC's competitive position in product. What the stockholders were told in the report was, "Planned capital expenditures for the next two fiscal years exceed $100 million annually."

Stockholders should have been nervous over that amount, for it far exceeded any new product spending ever before attempted at AMC. In the report, Luneburg and Chapin are posed in front of the two newest AMC products, the 1974 Jeep Cherokee, which was to become the fast-selling new sport utility and eventually the best-selling Jeep of all time, and the other, the all-new Matador coupe, which was the vehicle that eventually ran AMC out of business. Chapin and Luneburg didn't know it at the time, but with the introduction of the Matador coupe, the end of AMC as an American car builder was within sight.

Chapter 5

1974-1977
The Die is Cast

Over the past few years some historians, those who cared to, have submitted their written opinion as to where AMC made its fatal wrong move, whatever that was -- the sole and single mistake or poor decision that cost it its life as an independent company.

Many of these opinions have been made in magazine articles, usually as an aside to the main subject of the article, and few have been well researched or carefully thought out. Many writers have pointed an accusing finger at the plainness of the Rambler cars of the late fifties, or the lack of a performance image in the middle part of the sixties, or at the impact of the wave of compact car competition that surfaced within the seventies. While there is a bit of truth to some of that and no truth in most of it, it is easy enough to find instances of real failure in the American Motors story. The number of automotive flops is not high in AMC history because it couldn't have lasted as long as it did if it continually produced poor-selling cars. The Marlin stands out as a poor-selling, poorly styled car. The second generation of the Javelin sold poorly, but that was mostly because it had followed the rest of the industry and gotten too big and too expensive to appeal to the young, single people at which it was supposed to be aimed. The car itself was styled reasonably well. However, in 1974, AMC did come out with a car that has to be considered a failure, and a big one at that.

The market itself turned on AMC in the late 1970s. The American car market has been notoriously unkind to the smaller automakers. The very wonder of AMC is that it outlasted all the other independent automobile makers to become, by the end of 1966, the last independent. The struggle to survive had been a tough one in 1967, but then again this was one tough company. In the end a combination of good cost controls, tight tooling budgets, interchangeability of parts and all the other myriad good business practices it had learned along the way kept AMC afloat until the market turned again in their direction.

In the 1974-1977 time frame, it all seemed to unravel. The industry itself, fat after a record-setting year in 1973, ran into problems in 1974 as a recession and inflation worked hand-in-hand to create a downturn in auto sales.

The only really new car in the AMC line for 1974 was the Matador coupe. Market research had told AMC officials that, although they were getting a share of the intermediate size four-door sedan and station wagon market with the bulky but well made Matador, the hardtop version was not getting its fair share of the exploding mid-size two-door market. The reason, according to the analysts, was that the Matador hardtop was too conservatively styled. In truth, the hardtop Matadors were just too far off the beaten path style-wise. The Oldsmobile Cutlass was the hottest car in the mid-size market, with the stylish Chevy Monte Carlo and Ford Torino top sellers as well.

The decision was made to restyle the two-door Matador into a high profile, high-style mid-size coupe to compete directly against the best of the Big Three. A crucial part of the design program that was eventually agreed on was to style the Matador coupe completely as its own model, that is to say, not to share any tooling of the coupe with any other models of Matador. This was a risky move and went against every lesson that history had thus far taught AMC.

Many argued for the program, pointing out that being free to design the new car as a pure coupe would allow the designers flexibility to design a truly exciting machine, one that would have no visual ties to a mundane sedan. Although the Hornet/Gremlin program had used interchangeability as its foundation, it was felt that styling was a more important element in the mid-size coupe market, and to a large extent that was true. The Olds Cutlass Supreme was a hot-selling car because it was a beautiful car, exactly what the market wanted both in size, appearance and image. Now AMC styling wanted the chance to do what Olds designers had done, style a single model solely as a coupe, and make it as pretty and exciting as metal can be made to look.

Roy Chapin gave them that chance and the resulting new car, the 1974 Matador coupe, was pictured in full color on the front cover of the 1973 AMC annual report. Inside, smiling Chapin and Luneburg stood in front of the new car and the new Jeep Cherokee. The Matador was also featured on the front cover of the AMC new car brochures, which showed and explained the features of the new mid-size, as well as the rest of the AMC line of cars. Another front cover spot for the new Matador was the November 1973 issue of *Car and Driver* magazine. There, a fire engine red coupe, trimmed in sporty Matador X stripes and wheels, was featured with this headline: "1974's Best Styled Car."

The styling certainly caught one's attention, no question about that. Built on a wheelbase of 114 inches, the new coupe surprised a great many people by its bold new look. The car was offered in three models: coupe, Brougham coupe, and "X" coupe. Standard engine was the reliable old 232 cid six for the coupe and Brougham, 304 cid V-8 for the Matador "X." As was the practice in Detroit cars of the seventies, the standard equipment list was short while the option list was long. Thus, base coupes got E78 x14 bias-ply blackwall tires as standard, along with three-speed manual shift, non-power front disc brakes, and dog dish hubcaps. Radio, power steering, automatic transmission, and air conditioning were all on the option list. Brougham models came with full wheel covers, extra chrome moldings, and a nicer interior.

But the styling was a bit odd. Teague's men had fashioned a large coupe that had a close coupled cabin fronted by what appeared to be the longest hood in history. And nestled in that front end were two deeply tunneled headlights as well as a plain recessed grille. The rear quarter windows were

186

Matador Brougham

AMC BUYER PROTECTION PLAN

1. A simple, strong guarantee!

When you buy a new 1974 AMC car from an American Motors dealer, American Motors Corporation guarantees to you that, except for tires, it will pay for the repair or replacement of any part it supplies that is defective in material or workmanship. This guarantee is good for 12 months from the date the car is first used or 12,000 miles, whichever comes first. All we require is that the car be properly maintained and cared for under normal use and service in the fifty United States or Canada and that guaranteed repairs or replacements be made by an AMC Dealer.

2. A free loaner car from almost every one of our dealers if guaranteed repairs take overnight.

3. Special Trip Interruption Protection.

4. And a toll free hot line to AMC Headquarters.

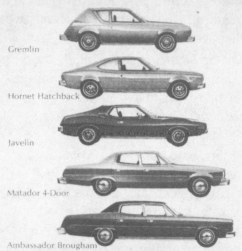

Gremlin

Hornet Hatchback

Javelin

Matador 4-Door

Ambassador Brougham

PRESENTING THE ONLY ALL-NEW MID-SIZE CAR FOR 1974

Matador X

AMC ▚ **Matador**

1974 Matador coupe with excessively long hood and deep tunneled headlamps.

teardrop shaped, the rear roof ended in a fastback, and the doors had frameless windows. It was startling, and yet it also seemed to give a case of deja vu. It looked for all the world to be an updated Marlin.

The Matador sedans and wagons were still in the lineup, although they were very much second fiddle to the Matador coupe. They were mostly carryover with the exception of a regrettable restyling of the hood and grille that makes one wonder who on earth could have ever decided to waste money tooling for it. The hood was made longer in the center, to make the entire car appear longer, while the edges of the hood tapered back to meet the existing fenders, which were unchanged from the prior year. This served to give an ungainly look that many wags called the "Jimmy Durante snout," which certainly was not the sort of talk a company wants to hear. The grille itself consisted of two opposing loops that ran around the inside edges of the new snout, giving it a curious, almost cross-eyed look.

The reason for the poorly executed face-lift of the sedans and wagons was the tremendous expense of retooling the Matador coupe. The program cost was enormous, but the resulting car was supposed to sell in large numbers, and at a greater per piece profit than the Hornets and Gremlins. In the meantime, the sedans and wagons would have to wait until enough money was available to restyle them as well.

Like the Matador sedans and station wagons, the Gremlin was mostly a carryover product for 1974, although it was now going into its fifth year on the market without a change. The grille was new, a more expensive looking piece of plastic that gave a slightly longer look to the car. The bumpers were new in response to new federal regulations that called for better protection in low-speed crashes.

Hornets were mostly carryover as well, but that was considered a safe move since the Hornet, as well as the Gremlin, had both sold so well in 1973. Javelin and AMX were similarly held to a minimum of changes. The Ambassador series was simplified for 1974, with the two-door hardtops no longer offered. That body style had always been shared with the Matador, and since the Matador hardtop was gone, so too was the Ambassador. No Ambassador version of the Matador coupe was ever considered. The big Ambassadors got a handsome face-lift, using the same elongated hood as the Matador sedan but with a better integrated theme for the grille, which was cleaner and carried quad headlights. Ambassadors came in four-door sedan and station wagon styles, in a single Brougham series.

Looking back on the models offered, it's obvious that the big emphasis for 1974 was on the new Matador coupe. Estimates vary, but it's a safe bet that about $40 million were spent on tooling for the coupe. The cost to the corporation was even higher, for the money spent on the new Matador meant that the Gremlin/Hornet series would have to wait for two more years before any funds could be released for restyling them. A new compact car was already planned for 1975, so the Gremlin/Hornets would have to soldier on in the market wearing their existing looks until 1976. By then, profits from the new Matador and the new car for 1975 should put AMC in clover. Things could really be happening.

Things were happening at Jeep as well, but they had a more positive effect on the futures of the company. The Jeep Renegade package, a hot-selling dress-up option on the CJ series, was finally made available on a full-year basis instead of on a limited basis as in past years. A new full-sized four-wheel-drive station wagon model, the Cherokee, was offered in an attractive two-door style that happened to be just what the public was hungry for, and they bought it in droves. The Cherokee was

New Cherokee

It's a Jeep and-a-half

The newest Jeep₂ vehicle has arrived. Jeep Cherokee. Heir to a tradition of quality and rough road dependability, Cherokee takes up where Jeep CJ-5 leaves off. Youthful and sporty, with the extra room that lets you pack along what you used to leave behind.

Cherokee really stands out where the pavement ends because the famous Jeep 4-wheel drive was specifically designed into Cherokee—most of the competition are merely converted two-wheelers. With greater ground clearance and a higher load capacity than any other sports utility vehicle in its weight class, new Cherokee makes a big difference in the boondocks.

Jeep Cherokee combines this rugged performance with sporty good looks—plus exciting options like Quadra-Trac, Jeep's automatic 4-wheel drive, automatic transmission, power steering, air conditioning and power front disc brakes.

New Jeep Cherokee is the get-away machine *your* family has been waiting for. It's a Jeep-and-a-half.

Jeep Cherokee
From A Subsidiary of
American Motors Corporation

For 1974, Cherokee, built on the Wagoneer chassis, replaced the Commando as the mid-sized Jeep vehicle. Originally only this narrow-wheel two-door was offered.

189

offered as a four-wheel-drive two-door wagon with various trim options to dress it up as fancy as the buyer wanted. Advertising called it "A Jeep and a Half." Since the Cherokee was essentially a two-door version of the Wagoneer, that model got a new grille and began a move further upscale to avoid direct competition with the Cherokee.

The 1974 product plan seemed sound, and some ex-AMC managers might still think it was sound, but in it lay the seeds of AMC's eventual failure. You couldn't see it in the 1974 annual report, but it was there nonetheless. The annual report to the stockholders showed that AMC domestic passenger car sales went up slightly to 385,000 from 380,000 in 1973. Market share took a big jump to 4.7 percent from 3.8 percent. Jeep sales set another record, 72,000 units in the United States. Unit sales outside the United States were also up to 95,794 units of combined AMC/Jeep, up from 67,374. Even AM General was up a tad, to dollar sales of $159 million.

It all looked pretty good, except when one looked at the financial numbers. There, it was bragged that AMC had total sales revenues of $2,000,200,000, topping the $2 billion mark for the first time ever. But operating earnings dropped to $27.5 million, and this time there was no tax-loss carryforwards or extraordinary credits to pump it back up. Thus, the operating earnings of $27.5 million were also the net earnings, and that was down from $85.9 million in 1973, a huge drop by any measure, but especially damaging since it occurred on sales of 552,000 units. What, one might have wondered, would happen to profits if sales decreased?

Working capital also declined to $157,037,000. Although that was still a large and comfortable amount of cash, it must be remembered that this was a period of higher inflation, and a dollar didn't buy as much as it had before.

As Chapin and Luneberg pointed out, the lower profits had been a result of heavy losses at AM General, which was experiencing problems in launching its new Transit buses, and also by a strike at the Kenosha auto plant that caused a $13 million drop in profits all by itself. AMC car sales were up slightly in a year when the industry had dropped 20 percent, but the marketing costs had increased because of the distress pricing in effect at the competition.

But one cause of the lower earnings was the expense of tooling for the Matador coupe. Matador sales did indeed increase, from 55,960 in calendar 1973 (which includes some early 1974 sales) to 77,720 in calendar 1974. Production figures show an even more dramatic and probably better illustrative set of numbers. The 1973 model year run of Matadors was 52,532 total. The 1974 model saw 99,586 Matadors built. Those numbers include all body styles of the Matador series -- coupe, sedan and station wagon. They were not really what had been expected, for the program cost was high, and the new car had to sell higher volume than just 77,000 cars. Because so much cash had been lavished on this one body style, a style that could never be translated to a four-door sedan or station wagon, the coupe itself had to sell over 80,000 units with the other Matadors adding perhaps 35,000 more units to the total.

It was hoped that sales would continue to grow year by year to bring in the higher profit margins that had been the sole reason for getting into the specialty coupe market in the first place. In the meantime, the stockholders were treated to a teaser photo of the nameplate of the next all-new car from AMC. Since the Matador had not had real success in 1974, the new 1975 compact car would have to be a hit or things were going to start to unravel at AMC. The 1974 annual report had a color shot of a section of hood of the all-new compact car that proudly wore the name of the car that was sure to bring prosperity to American Motors ... the Pacer.

The Pacer was the new entry in the small car segment, in between the Gremlin and the Hornet.

The most unique car of the 1970s, the AMC Pacer sold very well in 1975, its first year.

Riding a 100-inch wheelbase, the same as the original 1950 Nash Rambler, Pacer was meant to be a boldly different approach to small cars, one in which interior room would be comparable with many intermediate-sized cars. Rounded styling featured a very short front end, a low belt line and an emphasis on large glass areas. The Pacer was a very startling vision indeed. The proportions were unlike anything ever before, a large body with an extremely short overhang. Tall, glassy and very modern looking, the key to Pacer room was its width. At 77 inches, it was wider than Gremlin or Hornet, wider even than the larger Chevrolet Nova or Ford Granada. Pacer was originally designed to include a radical new engine, the Wankel rotary engine. General Motors was designing the engine for use in several of its cars, and AMC planned to purchase the engine in volume for its new breed of small cars. It never happened as the fuel crisis proved one bad point about rotary engines: They didn't get very good gas mileage. Mazda was the only maker offering rotary-powered cars in America, and it was in deep trouble trying to sell their cars, which had reputations as gas hogs. Luckily, AMC was able to shoehorn its trusty 232 cid six into the engine bay of the Pacer, although it meant

191

redesigning the bulkhead, and it buried the rear spark plug under the cowl. The 258 engine was offered as an option; it fit anywhere the 232 could go. Pacer had a lot of new technology, at least new to AMC. Rack and pinion steering, rare on an American car at that time, was standard, with much needed power assist as an option. The radiator was a new cross flow type, the engine had electronic ignition, and overdrive was available as an option. Some old features were there as well. The standard transmission was a three-speed column shift, as a floor shifter was an option. The base brakes were drum, with disc an option. Cheap 6.95 x14 bias-ply blackwall tires were standard, and the only

The car that was the fulfillment of the AMC "Philosophy of Difference" has to be Pacer, introduced in 1975.

way to get overdrive was with the column shift stick. Four-speed transmissions, standard on every Japanese car, were not offered at all on Pacer, nor were five-speeds.

Still, looks are what usually sells cars, and Pacer had looks like nothing else anyone had ever seen. As with the original Gremlin, some older people were turned off by the Pacer's styling, but by and large, it was a smash hit stylewise. Car and Driver magazine featured the new car on the cover of the February 1975 issue and wrote pages of glowing tribute to the unique new compact. Sales, initially, were red hot. The United States car market was suffering another one of its down cycles, this one made worse by inflationary pressures on car prices. But the egg-shaped Pacer got people interested in cars, and AMC dealers reported big increases in showroom traffic. The customers weren't just looking either; they were buying the Pacer in record numbers. Designer Dick Teague was well pleased as he had championed the Pacer program, daring the company to take another risk on unique styling, in the spirit of their self-proclaimed "Philosophy of Difference." The Pacer came with an exceptionally long list of optional equipment, so the average car went out the door for at least $1000 more than the advertised price of $3299.

Gremlin sales fell sharply in 1975 due to an extremely poor market and dated styling.

The Hornet Sportabout for 1975 - The new "Touring Package," shown above, had a tan vinyl roof and back panel overlay.

In 1975, now entering its third model year, the popular Hornet hatchback received a new grille.

The rest of the AMC product line was carryover again. Gremlin and Hornet wore the same old styling, now six years old, and few mechanical changes. The Matador coupe now offered a poor-looking landau vinyl top, an admission that its fastback styling was already out of style. Matador sedans and station wagons got a new grille to replace the one introduced just the year before.

The Matador sedan for 1975 had a new grille but a dated profile.

Of more historical interest is what was no longer in the product range for 1975. The Ambassador was dropped as all big car sales would now be Matadors. The Javelin and AMX were gone as well. AMC explained that the line was being trimmed to allow more efficient factory utilization, but that was only partly true. The Javelin and AMX had been introduced in 1971, had never sold in significant volume, and by now were old designs competing in a shrinking market segment. There was no sense at all in redesigning them yet again as there was scant hope of ever generating a profit from them. It's curious that no attempt was made to build them on the Hornet chassis, which would have made them viable products, but corporate attention was focused on the new Pacer.

The Pacer was a first year hit, selling in large numbers and becoming the most successful first year car in AMC history. A total of 96,769 units were retailed in calendar year 1975. That was the only good news, as sales of the rest of the line dropped like a stone. The cause was the recession as the younger, lower income small-car buyers were the first to suffer a layoff from work, taking them out of the new car market. Too, consumer confidence was low, keeping people who had no danger of layoff out of the showrooms. Adding in the higher car pricing caused by newly mandated safety and emissions equipment, as well as inflation, it's easy to see why the market was so bad. New car sales for the industry had fallen from 11.8 million in 1973 to just 8.2 million cars in 1975.

AMC car sales took a big drop in the first half of the year before the March introduction of the Pacer. After Pacer came out, sales of the entire line picked up and the company slipped back into profitability. It was too late to save the year, however, and the company, despite a large increase in dollar volume, suffered a loss of $27.5 million, wiping out the prior year's profit. Net sales were $2,282,199,000, a healthy increase in a down market despite a drop in domestic retail car sales to 296,000, down from 385,000 the prior year. Significant was the fact that wholesale units to dealers fell less, down only 59,000 cars. This meant that dealers were now sitting on a large amount of inventory, and if sales didn't increase soon, the dealers would have to reduce their orders for new stock units. A rude awakening came when sales of the Matador were totaled. The results showed a big drop in deliveries instead of the hoped for increase. For the calendar year, 61,048 units were sold of all body types. Matador was outsold by Gremlin, Hornet, and Pacer, despite having newer styling than the first two and more body offerings than the latter car. Things looked bad.

For 1975, the Matador coupe showed new styled road wheels, added disc brakes and steel-belted radial tires to its standard equipment list.

Jeep CJ's
Built this tough for the fun of it

The rugged Jeep CJ's. Famous for their ability to handle the roughest terrain. And now available in CJ-5 and the extra convenient CJ-7. Both built with Jeep's classic 4-wheel drive know-how. So they work hard and play hard — and here's how they do it. **Extra rugged frame** with **six cross members** — for the strength and durability you depend on in rough driving situations. **Wide spaced springs and shocks** — for excellent lateral stability and control. **Quadra-Trac,** Jeep's exclusive automatic 4-wheel drive — the system that's unsurpassed by the competition — is optional on the CJ-7. So you get traction and power when you need it, automatically. No more locking hubs! **Open-end front axle** designed to give the CJ exceptional control in tight situations. Comfort options on the CJ-7 — **removable hard top** with **steel doors** and **roll up windows.** **Automatic transmission** is available on the CJ-7. **Longer wheelbase** on the CJ-7 — for a smoother ride in the rough and on-pavement. **Extra room** — The CJ-7 offers the space you need to handle more of your gear. The Jeep CJ's. Tough, rugged and durable, and with the advantages that make them better than ever — for the fun of it!

Jeep Corporation is a subsidiary of American Motors Corp

Jeep

Jeep wrote the book on 4-wheel drive .

CJ-7's longer wheelbase allowed enough room for optional automatic transmission and Quadra-Trac.

197

Top: As sales tumbled, the Sportabout struggled on into 1976 with no major changes. Bottom: Hornet sedan for 1976.

Against all the doom and gloom, Chapin fought back. Cost controls were tightened, new spending was cut, and plans were made to enhance the product position for 1976. Things had gone better at Jeep. Sales were down just a handful, more a pause in Jeep's continual sales increase than anything else. New products in the Jeep line would get them back on track.

For 1976, the Gremlin was positioned as the lowest-priced car made in America at a bargain $2889 for the basic sedan. A new tactic was tried for the Hornet lineup, as the sedans and the hatchback were now all priced the same, $3199, while the Sportabout was $3549. It didn't help all that much, as the problem with the Hornet and Gremlin had little to do with price. The Hornet/Gremlin lines were now entering their seventh year in the market without a reskin or redesign, and they just couldn't get anyone excited anymore. The Gremlin got a new grille center, hardly an exciting thing even if it was attractive, which it wasn't. Hornet, Matador coupe, Matador sedan and Matador stationwagons were all carried over with little that was new. The Pacer, the daring new car of 1975, also returned with not much new. Pacer sales were already starting to slow down as its newness wore off.

Now in its seventh model year, for 1976 the Gremlin's styling was getting stale. The grille and "X" stripes received yet another updating.

1976 Matador coupe with Barcelona interior.

At Jeep, things were more lively. For 1976, Jeep introduced a new CJ model, the CJ-7, to supplement the CJ-5. CJ-7 had a 10-inch longer wheelbase, which finally provided enough room for engineers to fit an automatic transmission. Quadra-Trac full-time four-wheel-drive was likewise newly available on the CJ-7, as well as an attractive fibreglass hardtop. It all added up to a more civilized CJ and opened up more of the sport utility market to Jeep. The Renegade package continued to be a big seller on the CJ line, and the Cherokee was prepared to continue its successful run.

Still, American Motors was primarily a car company, and if you're a car company that fields a collection of dated carryover cars that don't sell, then you know what comes next. American Motors lost money again in 1976, a lot of money this time. Dollar sales had increased to $2.3 billion from $2.2 billion, but that was inflation, really. Net losses for the year climbed to $46,340,000. That wasn't the biggest loss AMC had ever suffered, but it was a tough loss coming right after the $27.5 million loss in 1975. Working capital plummeted to $59.7 million, and that was an especially scary sight. The loss was entirely from United States passenger car sales, as Jeep, AM General, Wheelhorse Tractors, and all the other subsidiary companies that made up American Motors were profitable that year. Retail sales of AMC cars in the United States and Canada had dropped to 292,087 from 328,181 the year before. This year the annual report reported combined U.S. and Canadian unit

Top: 1976 Pacer D/L. Bottom: Pacer "X." Note the plain horizontal bar grille and tunneled headlamps.

201

The 1976 Matador Brougham coupe, with optional Barcelona package. Noted the painted wheel covers, Barcelona nameplate on hood, new grille and hood ornament.

sales instead of U.S. only sales, to lessen the sight of the dramatic decline in United States sales. It had already begun to highlight retail sales instead of wholesale sales, but would switch back to reporting wholesale sales again in the near future.

A far scarier sight was on the inside front cover of the annual report, in one of the few color photos that appears in that spartan document. The 1977 AMC cars were shown, and for the most part they again were a line of carryover cars. Money was so tight that no really new product could be tooled anymore. In fact, although no one knew it at the time, the 1975 Pacer would earn its place in history as the last all-new American Motors car. For 1977 and for the next 10 years, every new AMC car would be based on an existing chassis.

You have to give Chapin a hand for trying. For 1977, the AMC car lineup got a few worthwhile low-cost improvements. The Gremlin at last got some new metal. The rear hatch window was made larger and deeper, while the front end sported a set of new, and shorter, fenders. The grille was all new, and this time it was quite handsome. The X model got renewed emphasis with a new and very attractive side stripe. Gremlin prices started out at $2995 for a basic six-cylinder sedan. In January, a new Custom model that included a new four-cylinder engine was announced at $3248. The four-cyl-

Top: 1976 Matador sedan. Bottom: 1976 Matador station wagon, still a family favorite.

1977 Gremlin showed compact front end styling, a handsome grille and an enlarged hatch window.

inder engine was long overdue. AMC had spent its development money on things like the Matador coupe and the Pacer, and had neglected the four-cylinder market. Now, in a time of high fuel costs, the Japanese makes were taking more and more of the small-car market. Lacking the time to engineer its own engine, AMC instead purchased a complete engine design from Audi in Germany. The engine itself was a 2.0 liter, roughly 122 cubic inches, which was too small for most of the AMC lineup, but it was considered adequate for the Gremlin. One problem with the engine was excessive vibration, which AMC solved by using very soft motor mounts. These mounts served to disguise the rough vibrations of the 2.0 liter, but a look under the hood of an idling Gremlin could certainly cause one to wonder about all that rocking going on. A bigger problem with the new four was that it cost more to build than the old 232 cid engine, in a car that was in the lowest price segment in the market. AMC solved that problem by offering the 2.0 liter only in the dressier Custom series, leaving a rock bottom six-cylinder sedan as the price leader. The Custom was available as a six-cylinder model as well.

Pacer got a new companion model, a smart station wagon. The station wagon was a two-door, like the sedan, but had a longer, squarer and more funtional rear end. The styling of the wagon was a bit more conservative than the sedan, and sales started out strong. Hornet also got a new model in the line, the Hornet AMX. Hornet AMX was the old hatchback model with a full dress-up package that

204

The new Pacer station wagon for 1977 revived Pacer sales for a while.

The 1977 Hornet AMX had wide, brushed aluminum "Targa" band, wheel flares and rear window louvers.

Top: The last year for the tired Hornet: 1977 Hornet sedan. Bottom: 1977 Hornet station wagon.

added wheel flares, rear window louvers, sport wheels, a brushed aluminum "targa" band on the "B" pillar, and an oversized hood decal.

The rest of the Hornet line was again carryover with a few touches to try to stir interest. More emphasis was placed on the D/L trim option, and all the cars in the catalogs wore sporty wheels or wheel covers. The Matador coupe was more garish this year; two-tone paints abounded. The Matadors now carried more standard features; power steering, power brakes, full wheel covers, automatic transmission and reclining seats were all standard equipment now.

1977 Matador coupe.

It all added up to a poor attempt to compete in the rough and tumble U.S. market. The Gremlin face-lift, while attractive, came to market at least three years later than it should have. The Hornet was badly in need of a complete reskinning; it looked ancient compared to the rest of the compacts on the market. The Matador coupe was dead; nobody wanted to buy it. The styling, which had appeared somewhat passe even when it first came out, now seemed incredibly stale. The Matador sedans and station wagons still sold in fair numbers, solely because of their superior value for the money. They remained in the lineup only because their tooling had long since been amortized, and they were reasonably cheap to build.

The Pacer station wagon, while attractive, could not offset the dramatic sales decline that the Pacer sedan had suffered. Pacer had sold well only in its first year when it outsold projections and

Top: 1977 Matador sedan. Bottom: 1977 Matador station wagon.

1977 Hornet hatchback.

Pacer's sales dropped further in 1977. Note the two different wheel treatments.

became the most successful first-year car for AMC. In calendar year 1976, Pacer retail sales had dropped to just 79,898, and Matador sales had dived to just 35,345. AMC had tried to jump start sales all during 1976. It hadn't worked, and it didn't work in 1977 either.

The Jeep line was hot, as it had been for a few years now. The Cherokee line, which had added a wide wheel Chief model in 1976 after a limited run in 1975, now added a four-door Cherokee as well. This was done at no cost to the corporation as the Cherokee four-door used the Wagoneer body and was simply a younger, sportier version.

The Wagoneer was aimed at the top of the luxury four-wheel-drive station wagon market, and it had that part of the market all to itself.

There was plenty of change in the company in 1977. Early in the year Eugene Amoroso, vice president of marketing, resigned. It could have been expected after the dismal sales results of the two previous years. In February the company celebrated 75 years in the car business, which it dated to when the first Rambler had been sold at the 1902 Chicago Auto Show. That Rambler had been built by the Thomas P. Jeffery Company of Kenosha, Wisconsin, one of the predecessor companies that eventually evolved into AMC. In May, AMC executives made an unusual effort to sway public opinion and reassure stockbrokers when it assembled a collection of small car prototypes from its styling studios and brought them to major cities throughout the United States to show opinion-makers the depth of design capability and expertise still within the company. Called "Concept 80," the prototypes were viewed by thousands.

Also in May, William Luneburg, president of the company, retired. This was an ordinary retirement, not forced, as Luneburg had reached retirement age. He was replaced by Gerald C. Meyers, one of Chapin's longtime aides and the man who had advised against buying Jeep in 1970. Another longterm employee, Iain Anderson, was elected executive vice president and chief financial and administrative officer. This put Meyers and Anderson in competition to win the chairman's seat someday. Both men reported directly to R.W. McNealey, vice chairman. Dale Dawkins was named to succeed Amoroso as vice president of marketing.

In August, AM General landed a huge order for military trucks. The trucks were a new type for AM General, 50,000 to 75,000 GVW heavy-duty linehaul tractors. The trucks were based on an existing truck built by Crane Carrier Corporation, which agreed to supply AMC's assembly line. A total of 5500 units were ordered, valued at $252.7 million, with an option to increase the order to over 8000 vehicles and $500 million.

In October, about 50 brand new Matadors were run through a used car auction in an odd attempt to reduce factory inventory of the model. Also in October, Roy D. Chapin relinquished his title of chief executive officer, in effect turning over control of the company to Gerry Meyers. Chapin remained as chairman, but it was clear he would soon be completely out of the action.

And in November, it was announced that a new joint venture plant in Egypt would build Jeeps for the Arab market. There was a bit of minor controversy by the Arabs, who wanted to blacklist Jeep because it had a distributor in Israel, but in the end it was decided that a Jeep plant in an Arab country was too good a deal to pass up, so it was allowed. The new plant, of which AMC owned 49 percent, had a capacity to build 12,000 Jeeps per year from parts made in America.

But American Motors was still primarily an automobile maker, and in the end it would live or die on car sales. For the fiscal year, retail sales of cars dropped again, down to 226,640 for the United States and Canada, from 292,087 the year before. AMC was again lumping Canada and the United States together to lessen the impact of the terrible sales results. Jeep sales were up again, to 117,077

Concept AM Van was a bit garish, subcompact size mini-van. Concept Grand Touring was Hornet-sized car. Styling was reminiscent of later Honda Accord.

Roy D. Chapin, Jr.
Chairman of the Board
American Motors Corporation
cordially invites you to
a showing of
Concept Cars for the 80's
at the
New York Hilton Hotel
Rhinelauder Gallery
New York City
Wednesday, June 1, 1977

4:00 to 6:30 p.m.   *R.S.V.P. enclosed card*

Invitation to concept cars for the '80s, AMC's traveling road show of prototype cars. This program was similar to the "Project IV" shows of the mid-'60s.

in North America. Although Jeep's international sales were also up, total international sales declined by 4700 units to 50,300 combined for car and Jeep, which proved that the drop in car sales didn't confine itself to North America. Car sales were down significantly in Mexico, a result of economic troubles in that country.

All the other divisions of AMC operated profitably for 1977. Wheelhorse, Mercury Plastics, and Evart Products were all in the black. AMC now listed car and Jeep as the Automotive Operations to signify that AMC was not only a car/truck builder, but a company that had other operations as well. These Automotive Operations, however, ran a loss of $1.2 million for the year. The results were actually much worse than that sounded as it showed that even hugely profitable Jeep couldn't cover the losses on car production. However, because the slim automotive group loss was more than offset by earnings from AM General and the other subsidiaries, American Motors was able to show an operating profit of $6.2 million, and, after allowing for income taxes and a tax credit, gave a net profit of just $8,266,000 on sales of $2,236,896,000, not much take-home pay for such a large amount of dollar volume.

Concept I was a sleek replacement for Gremlin. Concept II was of similar size, but had Pacer overtures.

It was a disappointment, this constant squeeze to turn a marginal profit, but it was a giant improvement over 1976's loss. It couldn't last, though. No car company can retool its product line when it is earning $8 million dollars a year. Tooling for an all-new car now cost at least $50 million if you were careful about it. In Europe, Ford had spent $1 billion to bring its all-new Fiesta to market. AMC was stuck in neutral at this point, too poor to afford a new car and sure to get hammered if it failed to introduce something new in the market. That was the problem AMC faced, and it came up with a reasonable response that had to win points for execution. For a ridiculously tiny sum, AMC planned to launch a new line of cars in a new market segment and expected to sell them in volume. There on the front cover of the annual report was the new small luxury AMC car, and it was a beauty. The new Concord was going to surprise a lot of people and give AMC yet another chance.

Chapter 6

1978-1984
The French Connection and the Brave New Jeep

As the 1977 model year ended, it was obvious that American Motors was in deep trouble. The opportunities of the mid-1970s were gone even as that hip age itself was coming to an end. The promise of high profits from the Matador coupe never happened as that model enjoyed one year of barely adequate sales, followed by three years of sales decline. The excitement that the public and press had displayed towards the revolutionary Pacer had fizzled out, apparently never to return. The Hornets were the best selling 1977 AMC car, but they, along with the Gremlin, were dying in the showrooms for a lack of new styling to rejuvenate them. Sadly, all of AMC's scarce capital had been spent on the Pacer and Matador, so the needed all-new designs for Gremlin and Hornet would never come.

Dick Teague and his staff designed an all-new mini subcompact to sell in the lowest price end of the market, but management decided against going in that direction. As Roy Chapin noted, "In the smallest cars, it got down to where we would have to redesign each and every part of the car, right down to the door handles and hinges to achieve the low weight needed, and we felt we were not in a position to get into that expensive a program." He was correct in that assessment. Teague also worked on a four-door proposal for the Pacer, but the Pacer was such an obvious flop that no more money was going to be pumped into that line. The Matador coupe was also a dead issue as it, too, wasn't selling. And the four-door Matador sedan and station wagons were still using the same old body. Roy Chapin doesn't remember any forward product designs for that line, nor does anyone else who worked at AMC at the time, so it's a safe bet that the entire Matador line was scheduled to be phased out sometime in the very near future.

That left the Hornet and Gremlin. Over the preceding years, a variety of proposals for restyling the Gremlin had been shown, some of them publicly at auto shows. An early study showed the exist-

217

In 1974, AMC unveiled this prototype, dubbed Gremlin G-II. Lines evolved into the Spirit liftback. Note color-keyed bumpers and the hatch-style rear window used instead of the regular hatchback door that Spirit had.

This Gremlin prototype, shown in 1974, had triangular shaped side window treatment, larger glass hatch and revised tail-lights. It's a shame the Gremlin did not get this handsome, low-cost redesign, as it cured the "closed in" feel of the rear seat area and improved rearward vision.

218

ing car with a redesigned sail panel incorporating triangular-shaped windows that retained the basic tooling while effecting a very different and attractive look. The design improved visibility as well. This redesign could have been tooled at a very modest budget, doing away with the claustrophobic feel of the rear seating area and increasing Gremlin sales. But the prototype only made it to the auto shows and was never put into production. Another Gremlin design study featured a storage bin that slid out from the rear cargo area and was dubbed the "Grembin." A sporty proposal done in 1974 showed a fastback rear and was dubbed the G-II.

But in the end, none of these had been built for production as AMC bet its future on Pacers and Matador coupes. The few poor dollars that AMC was able to invest in new product design for 1978 was only enough to slightly modify the Hornet body. Front fenders from the Gremlin were grafted

INTRODUCING AMC CONCORD

The luxury Americans want — The size America needs.

For 1978, AMC fortunes took a turn for the better with the introduction of the Concord.

onto the Hornet, with a new hood, very tasteful die cast grille, modified end caps on the rear fenders and new taillights. Engineering worked a miracle on the suspension, endowing it with a remarkably smooth ride that still allowed for above average handling for an American compact car. Sound insulation was liberally applied with the result a level of quiet unique for that size car. There were no changes to the drivetrain, save for whatever was needed to meet the latest emission standards. dards.

One very bright decision had been made: to move the Hornet line upmarket a bit, first by the smooth new suspension and quiet ride, and second by offering a dress-up option package. This clearly placed the car in the small luxury range and firmly out of the low-bucks market. The dress-up package was called D/L and consisted of a landau vinyl roof, individual reclining front seats, full wheel covers painted the body color (a la Mercedes), quartz clock (which was a rare and wonderful

AMC's chairman Gerald C. Meyers.

thing in 1978), wood-look dashboard, well trimmed door panels, and a host of other small touches that, at least for that time, clearly spelled out "luxury" to the average car buyer. So different was the feel of the car that it was decided to market it under a new nameplate, one that sounded more like a luxury car. The highly revised new car was thus named "Concord." Of course, by this time the Hornet name had lost most of the respect it had earned in the 1970-1974 time frame, so it was just as well that the name was retired.

The Concord, then, was a very plush auto and could be sold as a smaller, more economical family car. By reaching for that market, AMC could avoid direct comparisons of fuel economy with smaller cars from its competitors, and also avoid trying to compete head-to-head on pricing with the Big Three. And, of course, the Japanese makes were not in the same size category, so hopefully, decent sales and reasonable profits could be had. The success of the Concord was of critical importance, for the rest of the line would be carryover models yet again.

AMC's new president, Gerry Meyers, helped formulate a new strategic plan for the survival and growth of American Motors, and it was a good plan. Meyers felt he could restructure the company to take advantage of its strengths, minimize its weaknesses, and build a new company that would be highly profitable and less susceptible to the cyclical nature of the auto business. Roy Chapin was still the chairman of the board, but Meyers knew that Chapin's stay was going to be short-lived and that as soon as Chapin deemed it the proper time to step down and retire, he would do so. With all the losses of the recent past, now was just not the time to announce a new chairman.

220

But that was in the near future, and right now, today, AMC needed a hot-selling new car. It got one in the Concord. Dick Teagues' original Hornet shell had done wonders over the years, spinning off two-and four-door sedans, a hatchback and station wagon in the Hornet line, as well as a top-selling subcompact Gremlin. The body shell was now entering its ninth year of production, yet as the restyled Concord it became a desirable, handsome family car.

The best-selling model in the Concord line was the two-door sedan with a base price of $3749 and the optional D/L package that added $200 to that price. This $3949 price was up substantially from the price of the 1977 Hornet two-door, but the Concord was the much more handsome car, so much better trimmed that it was obviously a better buy. And that was what AMC was trying to accomplish with the Concord -- attract more people willing to spend a bit more money for a car that was a better value. The extra dollars that the customers were willingly spending on the new Concord were sorely needed by AMC to turn a profit. Roy Chapin said of the Concord, "...it's primarily a value-per-dollar car, meaning we have put a lot into that automobile and have raised the price relatively less than we might otherwise have done...." Chapin hoped to sell 80,000 Concords and later raised his expectations to 95,000-97,000 units.

The auto press liked the Concord well enough. *Auto Reports*, in its January 1978 issue, noted, "Our car had split bench seats in a beautiful crushed velour with fully reclining seat backs.... Noise levels are pleasingly low." *Auto Reports* summed up its test drive by stating, "All-in-all, the Concord is a big improvement over the Hornet, which was a pretty good car in its own right...." Although none of the buff magazines fell over in their praise of the Concord, virtually every auto tester came away impressed at the car's improvements. None, however, were impressed enough to feature the Concord on the cover of their magazine.

No matter, for the strong advertising schedule for Concord served to bring the folks into the showrooms, if for nothing else than a look. Once people drove the new Concord and compared its price to other domestic midsize cars, many agreed that Concord was a good value and decided to buy one.

It's a good thing they did because the rest of the line wasn't selling worth a darn. The Matador coupe returned yet again, showing off its optional "Barcelona" trim package that was almost offensively gaudy. The Matador sedan finally got a bit of attention when the "Barcelona" trim was offered on the sedan as well. Matador engine choices were trimmed down to just the 258 cid six-cylinder or the 360 cid V-8. At the slow rate at which Matadors sold, it was uneconomical to offer a wide range of power trains.

The Pacer line got some new touches as well, for all the good it would do. One theory that product planners had for the poor sales of the Pacer was its poor acceleration and lack of power. The product people translated customer complaints of inadequate power into a desire for a V-8 engine option for the Pacer, which was most certainly not what people wanted. The problem with the Pacer's power was not that the engine was too small, it was that the car itself was too heavy. The 232 cid six-cylinder engine was overtaxed by the sheer weight of the Pacer and felt anemic. The 258 cid engine was adequate, but just barely. True, AMC had not spent much time trying to pull more horsepower out of its sixes, as the primary concern at that time was fuel economy and emissions, but if the Pacer had been engineered for lower weight, its fuel economy and power would both have been more attractive to potential buyers. As it worked out, the Pacer received a 304 V-8 option for 1978, along with a curiously raised hood.

The new Pacer hood was meant to provide room for the new V-8 engine as well as a more conventional hoodline to placate some shoppers who complained that the front end of the Pacer was too low

In its final year, the Gremlin line for 1978 added this somewhat overdone Gremlin GT model.

and did not seem to offer enough protective hood space ahead of the driver. Too, it was now accepted at AMC that the style of the Pacer was turning off too many buyers, so Teague's crew attempted to please everybody by designing a new front end that would be more conventional, more protective, and even give a hint of the "Mercedes grille" that was so popular in America at the time. Instead of accomplishing all of those disparate goals, the pug nose Pacer received a Bronx cheer from the motor press, who realized the new look was an ugly mess.

The Gremlin, once the darling of the low-price market, was back for its ninth and final model year. Striping for the "X" package was revised yet again, this time less pleasing than the 1977 model. Value was the name of the game with Gremlin, as the $3539 base model now came with AM radio, whitewall tires, full wheel covers, and scuff moldings, all welcome additions. The little car had come a long way in nine years, almost doubling in price while still retaining the same overall look. The dashboard was all new and had a quality look to it, a vast improvement over the previous model. And a mid-year addition to the range was the Gremlin GT, a $649 option package that included fiberglass body flares and loud graphics. It was all for nothing, as the tired Gremlin just couldn't cut the mustard anymore, and slow sales only proved that.

There was one further spin-off from the standard Hornet chassis for 1978, and that was the AMX. The 1978 AMX was simply a revision of the 1977 Hornet AMX, sporting the new Concord front end, its own distinctive grille, and more flares and flash than most people would care for. The prior year's AMX had proven more popular than AMC expected, so for 1978 it was continued as a separate model.

And that was it for AMC cars; not much of a model lineup when one thinks about it, but it was all they had, and they would have to make the best of it.

There certainly were no problems with the Jeep line for 1978. Jeep was still riding the wave of high consumer demand for sport utility vehicles, and AMC could easily sell every Jeep they could build. The one problem developing at Jeep was a result of the incredible demand for the product, and that problem was a tendency to overlook quality control in the rush to build more and more Jeeps. The problems had little to do with reliability or safety, but quite a bit to do with customer satisfaction issues, things such as poor paint jobs, rattles, knobs and switches that fell off too soon.

Still, the problems with quality at Jeep were problems that all the builders of sport utilities were experiencing as the urge to sell more and more vehicles overcame the desire to build them well. Jeep sales for the year hit another record as demand continued to grow.

The annual report for 1978 summed it up best when it called 1978 "A year of progress on a strategic plan to make American Motors a well managed, growing, profitable world automotive company." It certainly was a year of progress, as the new Concord managed to slow the rate of losses in passenger car sales. It was too much to ask one new car, based on a nine-year-old design, to turn around a whole company, and wholesale sales of cars suffered another down year: 214,537 units worldwide compared to 227,365 units worldwide in 1977. But the loss had come in its older models: Pacer, Matador, and Gremlin. The Concord itself was a hit, selling 131,000 cars at retail in the United States and Canada, a 60 percent increase over the 1977 Hornet. For pocket change, AMC had created a hot new car.

U.S.-only sales of cars show more clearly where the market went for AMC. There, Concord sales for the calendar year were 114,764 vs. 79,508 1977 Hornets, while Gremlin slid to 24,412 from a weak 37,531 the prior year. Pacer sales were halved, 20,811 from 44,874, while the Matador dropped to just 9,471 units, less than a thousand per month, and that was for all body styles, not just two doors. The Matador coupe, "1974's Best Styled Car," was dead in the water.

Jeep wholesale deliveries in fiscal 1978 were 152,396 units in North America, a 31 percent increase from 1977, while overseas Jeep sales declined a bit, down 2,052 units to 28,271. Surprisingly, AMC car sales overseas increased, mostly due to a period of high prosperity in Mexico, where AMC was a medium-priced, highly popular car.

For the year, AMC sales rose to $2,585,428,000, up a gratifying $348,532,000. Profits were fair, $36,690,000. The profits came mostly from sales of Jeeps, as had been the case the prior year. In October 1978, Roy D. Chapin Jr. retired as chairman of the board, and Gerald Meyers took over as chairman and CEO. Meyers was already putting into action the plans that he, Chapin and the board had formulated to put AMC back in control of its destiny.

Firstly, it was recognized that the basic problem with AMC was too little demand for its cars, while the problem with Jeep was too little supply of the hot-selling four-wheel-drives. Since the plants could build more cars than were needed and not enough Jeeps, it was decided to convert some of the excess car production capacity to build Jeeps. Thus, the Brampton, Canada factory, which Chapin had arranged to buy so many years before, was converted from building Concords to building CJs. That move cut automobile overhead substantially, as did the closing of the ancient Milwaukee AMC plant. All AMC cars for North America would now be built at the Kenosha main plant, which would be operating more efficiently now that it was the sole car plant. The effect of the lower automotive overhead greatly affected AMCs profitability. Further, the new supply of Jeep CJs would add further cash to the bottom line since the Jeeps carried a much higher profit margin.

A key element to AMC's plans for the future was to concentrate on higher line cars, like the new

Top: Pacer wagon for 1979. Bottom: Pacer hatchback soldiers on despite poor sales.

Concord, which allowed for a better margin and were less susceptible to cut-price selling.

For the 1978 annual report, Gerry Meyers introduced the team of executives that he planned to use in his tenure as captain of AMC. He threw a curve ball when he announced that W. Paul Tippett, executive vice president of the Singer Company, was AMC's newest president. How a sewing machine executive fit into a car company was a good question until it was explained that Tippett had previously worked at Ford Motor Company in its hugely successful European operation. Also new to the company were Wilson Sick Jr., group vice president of finance and administration, and James L. Tolley, vice president of public relations. Tolley was recruited from Chevrolet, while Sick held an executive position at Bell & Howell. Sick had been brought in to replace Iain Anderson, who had quit to sign on with Volkswagen.

With the extremely capable Cruse Moss in charge of AM General, Stuart Reed as group vice president of operations, Lawrence Hyde as vice president in charge of car and Jeep vehicles, it was a solid and talented management team, one that Meyers said he was "willing to go to war with." A good question that wasn't asked at this point was exactly what qualities Paul Tippett had that interested Meyers. Tippett's service at Ford had been mostly in Europe, where he still maintained contacts. What Meyers now needed was a man who was well-versed in European automakers, although that certainly wasn't generally known at the time. It would slowly become clear in the near future.

The plans for the future were in the message to the stockholders, but it was somewhat vague to a casual reader. It read like this: "We have put our house in order so we can proceed with a fundamental part of our strategic plan -- to become a member of the group of worldwide auto companies that will be competitive in the years ahead. During 1978 we have conducted intensive negotiations in this regard with Renault." Worldwide auto companies? What did that mean? And exactly what was being negotiated with Renault?

Actually, the strategic plan for AMC was to form a working arrangement with an overseas automaker wherein AMC would be allowed to assemble one of that partner's small, fuel-efficient cars in its Kenosha plant. This would save AMC the expense of tooling for an all-new car, one that had all the weight-saving designs so common in imports. It was going to have to be done this way as the cost of tooling now was so high that it could bankrupt AMC even if the car was successful in the market. AMC had learned from its experience with the Metropolitan that it had to build the car in its own plants versus merely retailing a built-up import if it wanted to make an adequate profit. Meyers, at this point, held scant hope that the regular line of AMC cars could be made competitive without a high volume, high gas mileage car also in the lineup. There were going to be new AMC cars for 1979, 1980 and 1981, but although they would be small, fuel efficient cars, they would not get the sort of gas mileage that would be needed to compete in the volume part of the market. For that, an all-new, very different sort of car was needed.

Negotiations had started earlier with Roy Chapin. Chapin met with Honda and Peugeot, but things didn't click, and no agreements were made. Later meetings with Renault yielded more hope, for although the Frenchmen were tough negotiators, history was on their side. For many years, in far-off markets such as Argentina, and Mexico, Rambler and Renault had been able to work together to their mutual benefits. But, at the end of 1978, talks were still ongoing, and where they would lead was anyone's guess.

As the 1979 model year opened, there was plenty to feel good about at AMC. Dick Teague had pulled another one of his minor miracles of design when he restyled the roof, grille and back panel of the Gremlin, transforming it into the very attractive Spirit liftback. A second model in the Spirit

Top: Although based heavily on the Gremlin, the 1979 Spirit looked all new and very contemporary. Bottom: The influence of the 1974 G-II is obvious.

range was the Spirit sedan, which looked more like a Gremlin but with redesigned side windows and grille. Engineering worked some magic on the suspensions, much like what had been done the prior year on the Concord, so the Spirit had a smooth and quiet ride to go along with its sharp new looks. Base price was $3899 for the sedan, $3999 for the liftback. Both models came with the 2.0 liter four, four-speed, and bucket seats, so in specifications they were just what the market said it wanted. They were what AMC needed as well, for they represented new cars pulled from a common, existing chassis instead of another risky try at expanding the model range by getting into another expensive tooling program.

The launch of the Spirit was not handled with any of the skill that the Concord launch had shown. The car vied for attention in one ad with a couple running through the grass under the headline, "Let the Spirit move you." Wordplays like that were out of touch in the hard knuckle automobile market of 1979. The pricing was also mishandled. AMC had counted on the $3999 price to bring people in the door, and it did. But when the prospects got to the dealer, they found a lot full of cars with sticker prices in the high $5000 range up to the $6500 range, and that clearly was more than they wanted to pay. It was a common enough mistake for those inflated times, and the problem was that the first few thousands of Spirits sent to dealers were loaded with options that combined to pump up the sticker prices too high for the market. It was a case of poor judgment on the part of management, as the factory assumed that people would be willing to pay almost any price for a fuel- efficient small car. Maybe they had in the first gas shortage, but this time around customers were also being hit with high inflation, a very severe recession, high unemployment, and the highest interest rates on new car financing in history - about 16 percent. Additionally, a new term was now in common usage, "sticker shock," meaning the disbelief shoppers felt when they saw the price of a new car. Inflation was driving up sticker prices at a frantic clip, and if you had not bought a new car in four years, you were bowled over by the prices.

AMC recognized the problem fairly quickly when early sales results for the Spirit were not what they should have been, and the company reacted by reducing prices and adding some options onto the standard equipment list. That got things back on track, but time and sales were lost.

Concord was back, of course, with a new grille, new aluminum bumpers and some trim changes. Concord models now included the base series, a new D/L series that replaced the old D/L package, and a new high trim Limited series. The Pacer line now began with a D/L hatchback and station wagon and ended with the same two styles offered in Limited trim. There was an all new AMX built from the Spirit liftback body, and that was an attractive addition to the line.

The Matador line was gone. The lineup now included only small cars; 108-inch wheelbases or less. The dealers missed the old Matador wagon; it had always been a steady seller, but few missed the coupe. It had been a failure, and now it was consigned to history.

Jeep had no dramatic changes, but of course, none were needed as the Jeep line kept going from strength to strength. The Cherokee station wagon was still selling out, with waiting lists that ran to five months. The Cherokee line included several dressed-up models such as the Cherokee Chief, Cherokee S and Cherokee Golden Eagle. All the senior Jeeps received new front end styling with new grilles, front bumpers and rectangular headlamps. Renegade striping on the CJ was revised somewhat. A very special limited edition of the CJ came out mid-year -- the Silver Anniversary CJ -- to celebrate its 25th year of production. A special Silver Anniversary Concord was also put together to celebrate the 25th anniversary of the formation of AMC. Both of these limited-edition models were painted silver with special seat trim and commemorative badges.

Top: For 1979, AMX was based on the Spirit chassis rather than the Concord chassis, featured bold graphics and a choice of the 258 cid six or the 304 cid V-8. Bottom: 1979 Concord D/L two-door was handsome and popular.

Top: For 1979, the Concord D/L four-door received a vertical grille, quad rectangular headlamps, half-vinyl roof and new wheelcovers. Bottom: 1979 Concord D/L station wagon.

In January 1979, Gerry Meyers announced that the long-speculated agreement with Renault had been signed. The agreement called for AMC to begin, as soon as feasible, to distribute and sell Renault cars in the United States and Canada through its AMC/Jeep dealers. The first Renault offered would be the Renault LeCar, a thrifty but quirky front-wheel-drive sedan that was in the smallest end of the market. The plan called for AMC to add the new Renault 18 sedan and station wagon to its distribution network in 1980, to sell in the high volume compact market. Although the Renault 18 was similar in size to the Concord, they were so different in design that they would appeal to different buyers. Renault agreed to sell Jeeps in France and in Colombia, South America, two of the few countries where Jeep was not adequately represented in the market.

Analysts were at first disappointed, for the agreement did not call for AMC to assemble the Renault 18 in its U.S. plants. It was decided the Renault 18 was not the best choice for the high volume model that AMC needed to build, so instead an agreement was reached wherein AMC would provide imput on a smaller and even more fuel-efficient car that was still being designed, a model that was in- between the size of the LeCar and the 18. This new small French car was code named the X42, and it was planned to be introduced in the fall of 1982 as a 1983 model. This would be the culmination of the grand alliance that was being forged by AMC and Renault, a wonder of small-car technology.

This was what Meyers had meant when he got to talking about these world car companies. An all-new, front-wheel-drive small car with room for a family, good quality, and gas mileage in the high 30s was simply beyond the capability of AMC by the end of the seventies. The lost opportunities of the 1970s were coming home to roost now, and it can be said that the failure of the Javelin, Matador, and Pacer had cost AMC more than money. It had cost them their freedom; the ability to determine their future independently. From now on, most of the new cars from AMC would be designed in France by Renault to be sold by the AMC network.

The dealer network was the prize that Renault received in exchange for its small car designs. The existing Renault dealer network in the United States in 1979 consisted of about 250 small, undercapitalized dealers who sold Renaults usually as a second or third franchise. Sales were consistently under 18,000 per year and going nowhere. If Renault ever hoped to be a major force in America, it would need a better dealer body, and with the AMC network, it got one.

There was no talk of exchanging shares of stock in each other's company, no talk of a financial arrangement. Both AMC and Renault pointed out that this was an agreement, not a merger or buyout. Meyers, in an interview with *Wards Auto World* in December 1978, said this in response to a question of whether Renault would own any AMC stock: "We've said right from the beginning an equity participation in the company has never been in either one of our minds."

Meyers also stated to *Automotive News* in January 1979 that the agreement did not mean an end to the AMC line of cars. "Our AMC cars are set for 1980 and 1981 -- prototypes have been built, testing is underway, and production plans are proceeding."

As the year progressed, Meyers cancelled the agreement made with Audi to purchase its 2.0 liter engine plant. The decision had been made to offer a four-cylinder engine in the Jeep CJ series, and the little 2.0 liter, being a European design, didn't have the low end torque needed in a four-wheel-drive vehicle. A deal was made for General Motors to supply its 2.5 liter cast-iron four, an engine with enough torque to use in Jeeps as well as in the Spirit and Concord for the 1980 model year. AMC saved about $45 million in capital costs by cancelling the existing contract. Meanwhile, the Pacer stamping plant in West Virginia was sold to Volkswagen in a move to reduce automotive overhead. The way Pacers were selling, the plant wasn't needed.

In 1979, AMC became, for perhaps the first time, primarily a truck builder, as Jeep sales narrowly edged out car sales for the fiscal year that ended in September 1979. The car total had been enhanced by the addition of 13,000 Renaults, but in the end Jeep was the sales leader by a handful. It could certainly be argued that AMC already was primarily a truck builder since almost all of its recent profits came from Jeep, but for 1979 both unit sales and profits were more Jeep than anything else.

Of critical importance to AMC in 1979 was the second gasoline crisis. Gas prices rose as availability fell, and suddenly fuel economy and small cars were important subjects on the nightly news programs. The four-wheel-drive market peaked in March, then began to fall as buyers began to turn away from the fuel-thirsty sport utilities and began shopping for small cars. Jeep had such a large backlog of sold units that at first it seemed to be impervious to harm. But gradually, month by month, those sold units were built, shipped, and delivered, with fewer new orders coming in to keep the assembly lines going. By fall, AMC was facing a shortage of Jeep orders that forced production shutdowns to balance inventory.

There was no problem at AM General. Work began on the huge contract to build 6,549 of the giant M915 military trucks, as well as an additional 6,720 postal units.

In October 1979, an announcement was made that a further agreement had been signed with Renault wherein Renault would purchase five percent of AMC stock at $10 per share, along with subordinated notes and debentures that were convertible into AMC stock. The deal provided AMC with $150 million in cash, but eventually would give Renault 22.5 percent ownership of AMC.

What had happened to the statements of just a few months earlier that there would be no equity holding in either company? Suddenly, AMC had a senior Renault official sitting on its own board of directors. Another was scheduled to join the board in the future. The move was prompted by the high cost of tooling for the future joint project to build the new Renault small car in Kenosha. It was realized that all-new fixtures, tools and dies would be needed. Further, a major investment was going to be necessary for assembly robots, something AMC had few of. A great deal of money was going to be needed as working capital just to fund the supply of parts to the new assembly line, because this was going to be a very high volume entry in the market. Perhaps Meyers was also afraid of running out of cash before the new car was ready, for car sales were still not good, and sales of the Jeep line, lifeblood of the company, were not bouncing back.

American Motors ended its fiscal year in September 1979 solidly profitable. Total sales volume was $3,117,049,000, a record-setting year, with net profits of $83,944,000, the second best profits in its history. Of course, those were inflated 1979 dollars, so it really wasn't quite as good as it sounded, but it was good nonetheless. Wholesale unit sales of AMC cars for the fiscal year fell again, down to 207,557 units worldwide, and that number included some 13,460 Renault automobiles. At Jeep, wholesale units came in at 207,642, another solid increase for the year. Both cars and Jeeps had increased in overseas markets. Working capital was a heartwarming $235,876,000. It all seemed to be going well.

AMC was still operating on its traditional October to September fiscal year, which coincided with the traditional model year for car sales. This practice had been going on since the formation of the company, and was not, of itself, any sort of a problem. What was a problem was that this year, Jeep sales in the last quarter of the calender year 1979 had nearly come to a complete halt. Jeep dealers were glutted with a sea of unsold Cherokees and Wagoneers, units they had ordered months before and had still not sold. Since a dealer's inventory financing (called floorplaning) was set at normal

231

For 1980, AMC introduced the Eagle line of cars, the first four-wheel drive cars from an American maker. Two-door, four-door and station wagon styles were offered.

market rates, the Jeep dealers were being badly mauled by high finance costs on these unsold vehicles. The combination of high interest rates and slow sales were driving dealers into default in some cases. In the best of cases, it caused dealers to drastically cut their orders for new vehicles. Since American Motors was deriving nearly all of its earnings from Jeep, it was in a perilous position by the end of 1979. Yet the annual report didn't show that because it hadn't occurred within the 1979 fiscal year.

The 1980 Jeep line anticipated new concerns about fuel economy, but still the response was not effective enough. The CJ series now came with the 2.5 four-cylinder engine as standard equipment, as well as a four-speed transmission. The automatic transmission now came without Quandra-Trac, as that system was too fuel-thirsty. The 258 cid engine was optional as was the 304 V-8, although the latter was not very popular anymore. Free-wheeling front hubs, to disconnect the front axles when four-wheel-drive wasn't needed, were finally made standard, another fuel economy move. It all combined to make these the most fuel-efficient CJs in years. There was a renewed emphasis on Cherokee's six-cylinder engine, as well as the more fuel-efficient narrow wheel models. As with CJ, Cherokee now had a four-speed and free-wheeling hubs as standard equipment. Quadra-Trac was still optional, but a part-time four-wheel-drive system was more popular. Jeep put great effort into coming up with a dressy option package to lure buyers into showrooms, and the company introduced a Laredo package for CJ and Cherokee that was perhaps the most attractive option Jeep ever offered. Wagoneer had gas mileage improvements, as the 258 cid six-cylinder and part-time four-wheel-drive were made available to replace the standard 360 V-8 and Quadra-Trac.

Right on schedule, the 1980 AMC cars were announced in the fall of 1979. There was a new small four-wheel-drive car called the Eagle, which was the only new AMC car that fall. It really wasn't all that new as it wore the body of the Concord with a very advanced four-wheel-drive system. The Eagle was a right move by AMC for the times and was a remarkable achievement. For very little investment, AMC was able to enter the 1980s with a new type of small car, one with no domestic competition.

The Eagle represented everything AMC should have been trying to achieve in the car business. Use of a chassis and body shared with a regular two-wheel-drive car helped spread tooling costs around to the maximum number of units while saving on raw capital investment. Synergy was achieved in the use of Jeep engineers to work on Eagle's ride, handling, noise, vibration and harshness characteristics. The car itself was where AMC should be, in a market niche where its special abilities gave it an advantage over the bigger competition. A market existed, and probably still does, for a four-wheel-drive automobile that allowed the average driver to motor in safety regardless of weather or road conditions; a four-wheel-drive vehicle with the traction of a Jeep but the ride and comfort of an automobile. AMC expected to sell 35,000 Eagles, which carried a base price of $6999 for the lowest priced two-door sedan. Eagles tended to be sold with a high content of options, so the average price out the door was closer to $9500, a good piece of change even in 1980.

All Eagles in that first year came with power steering, power disc brakes, automatic transmission, six-cylinder 258 cid engine, and full-time four-wheel-drive. The system used a fluid coupling that sensed when a wheel was losing traction, and directed more power to whichever axle had the best traction. The system worked silently, smoothly, and was a very reliable set-up. Some off-road enthusiasts decried its lack of a low range in the transfer case, but its omission was deliberate. The Eagle was to be a four-wheel-drive automobile, suitable for some light-duty off-road driving, but not the sort that would need a low range gear.

The Eagle wagon was far and away the most popular model in the Eagle line. The "Sport" package shown had blackout chrome and a 4x4 decal on lower front door.

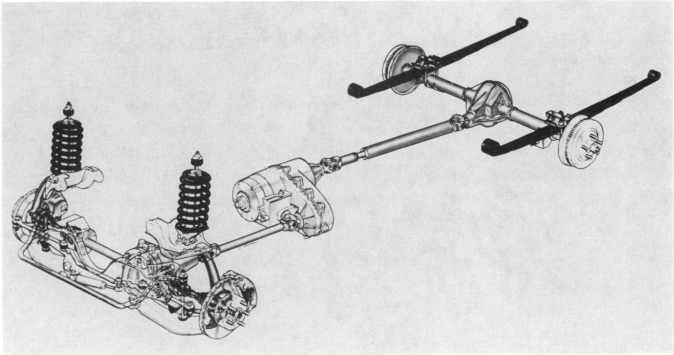

Top: Phantom view of the Eagle drivetrain layout. Bottom: Eagle suspension system. Note the independent front suspension and leaf spring rear.

235

The Eagle line consisted of the same two-door, four-door, and station wagon styles that the Concord had and appeared to be exactly the same. There were differences, but they were few. For one thing, Eagle bumpers stood closer to the body. Eagles were classed by the government as light-duty commercial vehicles, and didn't require, or have, five mile an hour bumpers. Too, Eagles stood about three inches higher on their chassis to provide clearance when driven off-road, and wore Krayton plastic wheel flares to lessen the "jacked up" look. Fifteen-inch tires and wheels with unique wheel covers were fitted to all Eagles.

The 1980 Concord had a few appearance and equipment changes, too. A new, rectangular opera window was used on two-door D/L and Limited series, while four-doors got a full vinyl roof and new quarter windows that were quite attractive. The Concord hatchback was no longer offered, as it had not been popular in 1978 or 1979. One of the watchwords of the Meyers' years was line "rationalization," wherein slow selling models were pruned from the lineup, and the Concord hatchback

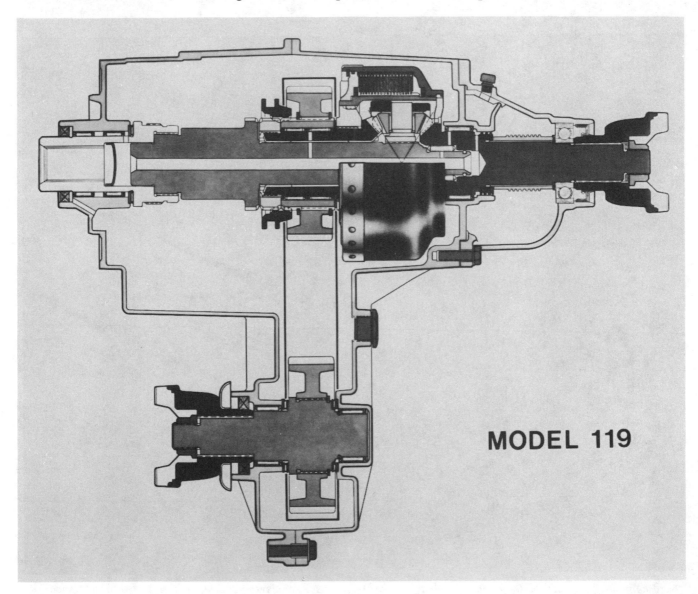

Eagle transfer case.

Top: 1980 Eagle two-door sedan. Bottom: 1980 Eagle four-door sedan.

The popular Concord D/L two-door for 1980 showed new landau vinyl top, revised grille and new taillights.

was one of the first casualties. The rest of the AMC line was carryover as the emphasis this year was on the new Eagle.

Mechanical changes were numerous and important. That old trusty standby, the 232 cid six-cylinder engine, was dropped as its power output was too similar to the standard four-cylinder. The 2.0 liter engine line was tranferred back to Audi as the General Motors 2.5 liter Iron Duke became the standard engine on Concord, Spirit, and Jeep CJ. The 258 cid six-cylinder engine became the only optional engine for the Spirit and Concord, as the 304 V-8 was no longer offered on cars. Pacer, Eagle and AMX were thus available with just one engine, the 258 cid.

Renewed emphasis was placed on the Concord D/L four-door for 1980, which received new taillights, grille and dramatic quarter windows, along with a full-vinyl roof.

All AMC brand cars came with factory Ziebart Factory Rust Protection, as AMC made improvements in manufacturing that reduced the chance of rust developing too early in the product's life. Ziebart Factory Rust Protection was a comprehensive program to combat rust and did not rely solely on the protective coatings applied to the underbody.

A quick look at the car line showed clearly that all the so-called volume models were based on the old Gremlin/Hornet chassis, with the exception of the slow-selling Pacer. It didn't take a genius to figure what would happen next. On Dec. 3, 1979, Pacer production ended for good. AMC issued a statement that the move was to allow an increase in Eagle production, but the true reason was that Pacer sales were so low it was time to cut losses again.

Still, it was true that the Eagle was a hit. The readers of *Car and Driver* magazine named it "Most Significant New Domestic Car." The Eagle was featured on the cover of *Popular Mechanics* magazine. *Four Wheeler* magazine placed it on their cover as well, and carried a glowing story inside, titled, "The Eagles Have Landed." Among other things, *Four Wheeler* noted "...comfortable ride is a goal AMC has achieved with the Eagle," and "...the ride is practically road-car smooth, and off road

1980 Concord station wagon received a revised grille and blackout side window trim.

AMX for 1980 came with just one engine choice, the 258 cid six.

the independent front and live rear team up to handle shocks, bumps, and lumps with ease."

AMC hiked production of Eagle to an annual rate of nearly 80,000 units, a very optimistic rate for the depressed market. In February 1980 the one millionth Jeep built by AMC, a CJ-5 Laredo, was produced. Also in February, it was announced that the first quarter of the 1980 fiscal year, October to December 1979, saw a 32 percent decline in operating income, down to $12.8 million from $18.9 million in the prior year's quarter. More ominous was that the results were down despite a 10 percent increase in dollar volume and a three percent increase in unit sales. Increased unit sales of Renault and AMC cars were offsetting the reduction in Jeep sales, but they were not as profitable. Paul Tippett was nonplussed, explaining that AMC was in solid financial shape. "Now," he said, "we're in a position where we can take some lumps and not get in the soup."

In April 1980 it was revealed that new, smaller versions of the Eagle were being readied for a fall introduction. Based on the Spirit line, these new Eagles would keep the momentum building. Because Jeep sales were so slow, it was decided to retool the Brampton plant back to car production and build Eagles and Concords there. The investment in retooling Brampton to Jeep was thus a loss, and the losses were just beginning. AMC was more dependent on Jeep sales than it had ever admitted, but it was fast becoming clear how dependent it really was.

All the previous plans went out the window. The scheduled increase in capacity at Toledo was ready to come on stream just as the market went down, so to offset that excess capability the Bramp-

241

Short model year. The 1980 Pacer hatchback (top) and station wagon (bottom) were in the AMC line-up at the fall introduction, but production ended by December 1979.

The 1980 Spirit sedan had carryover styling but received minor equipment changes.

Top: 1980 Spirit D/L liftback shown with optional "G.T." appearance package: Bottom: 1980 Spirit D/L in standard guise.

ton plant would have to stop building Jeeps. The plan to switch one production line in Kenosha from cars to Jeeps was also cancelled. By June, it was clear that even these changes were not enough. The company reported a loss of $84.9 million dollars for the quarter ending in June. This was the worse quarter in AMC history, worse than any full year loss the company ever had.

For the fiscal year ending in September, American Motors had to report a loss that was nearly beyond belief, $155,672,000. AMC chose this year to change its fiscal year to a calendar year basis, finally abandoning the old system of a fiscal year that coincided with the model year. That change made the loss even worse, as the sales decline was deeper in the second half of the year. For the calendar year, the net loss was $197,525,000.

What had happened to AMC had little to do with its product range. The recession/inflation team had knocked the American economy on its rear, hitting car sales with particular ferocity. Industry production of cars fell to 6.4 million units, down two million units from 1979, which was already down 1.2 million from the record 1973 peak. Truck production was also cut, to 1.59 million from

1980 LeCar. Although glass moonroofs and roof racks were available as dealer options, the factory-installed sunroof proved more popular.

2.97 in 1979. The industry was devastated, and all of the American automakers reported losses. As usual, though, the Big Three could sustain losses for a period of time while AMC could not. For a while, it was hoped that sales of AMC cars would pull the company through, but it was not to be. For the calendar year, 228,937 AMC and Renault cars were wholesaled to dealers worldwide, up a scant one percent from the 227,032 reported for calendar 1979. Jeeps sales for the period dropped to 98,871 from 191,172 for 1979, almost halved. Gerry Meyers tried to reassure the stockholders, speaking of a "Formula for the Future," but the staggering loss was on everyone's minds. In November 1980, AMC mailed a proxy to stockholders seeking approval of a plan to sell 20 million shares of AMC stock to Renault for $122.5 million, and convert its $45 million note to common stock, with a combined effect that would give Renault 46.4 percent ownership of AMC. That was difficult for the stockholders to swallow, but the alternative was "voluntary or involuntary" bankruptcy. Working capital had dropped to $94.6 million by September 1980, and the company was simply bleeding to death. Approval of the sale pumped up working capital to the $206 million figure shown in the annual report that year. Meyers pledged to spend $1 billion in the next five years to bring out new lines of Jeeps and cars. That sounded good to some folks, but to too many, it sounded like the same old song.

The 1980 Renault LeCar was popular among singles and young couples. Note the wheels bolted on with only three lugnuts.

So American Motors ended the first year of the 1980s by losing more money than it had ever lost before. Worse was that the only solution to its predicament seemed, at least to the man in charge, to be a sellout to a foreign company.

There was not too much new in the product lines for 1981 to give anyone hope about a quick turnaround. The Jeep line continued to show improvements in fuel economy. The four-cylinder CJ was

246

EPA rated at 22 mpg city/27 mpg highway. A new CJ pickup truck, called the Scrambler, came on a longer wheelbase and gave the company an entry in the hot compact pickup market, although it did not come in a low-priced two-wheel drive version. Sales of the CJ were not the problem. All Jeep sales were down to some degree, but Cherokee sales were hurt the worst by far. Cherokees were high margin/high volume units, the bread and butter of Jeep, and therefore of American Motors.

Intensive efforts were focused on improving fuel economy of the senior Jeeps, particularly in the drivetrains. The automatic transmission now had a lock-up torque converter. A front air dam was fitted to all Cherokees, Wagoneers, and J-series trucks. The J-series trucks had their roofs retooled to finally remove the lip over the windshield (a design touch dating back to the sixties) just to improve wind resistance. The downturn in sales did allow AMC a chance to improve the build quality of the Jeeps, and these were probably the best assembled units the factory had put out in years.

The AMC car line was further pruned by dropping the slow-selling AMX as well as the Limited models of the Spirit. Pacer, of course, had already been dropped. Two new models were offered in the Eagle line, the SX/4, which offered the Eagle drivetrain in a Spirit liftback body, and the lowest priced Eagle, the Kammback, which used the Spirit sedan, *nee* Gremlin body, and was priced at a bargain $5995 base. All Eagles came with the 2.5 four-cylinder as standard equipment in a bid to show higher fuel economy figures across the board. The tried-and-true 258 six-cylinder was the only option for 1981, but it was completely redesigned to improve fuel economy and reduce weight. The new engine still featured seven main bearings and all-iron design for durability, but now weighed 90 pounds less and got slightly better gas mileage. This new engine was fitted to the Jeep line as well, again for fuel economy.

There was big product news with the Renault line. The new 18i sedan and station wagon, first of the new volume Renault products, was introduced to great fanfare and a sales goal of 35,000-plus units. The 18i was a large compact size car, roughly similar to the Concord, but with product specifications that should have appealed to fuel-starved motorists that year. A fuel-injected four, front-wheel-drive and light weight all contributed to a gas mileage rating of 26 mpg city/37 mpg highway -- near the top of its class. With the smooth ride so typical of French cars, it offered room, ride, and fuel efficiency that should have made it an unqualified success.

LeCars came in for some revisions. Body colors were more conservative, an indication that AMC wanted the public to take the tiny car a bit more seriously. As could be expected, prices went up as well.

There were some highlights in the year. In March a coachbuilder in Florida announced convertible versions of the Concord and Eagle at a cost of $3975 plus the price of the car. Called Sundancer, they might have done better if the economy had been in better shape. Select-Drive, a major revision to the Eagle four-wheel-drive system, was made available. Select-Drive allowed a driver to disconnect the full-time four-wheel-drive system and run in just two-wheel-drive to increase gas mileage.

In June, Gerry Meyers stated that Renault would now handle all car design for American Motors. AMC engineers would work only on Jeep and Eagle designs. At this point several plans were being discussed, including basing future Eagle cars on Jeep chassis, or combining Jeep four-wheel-drive systems and Renault bodies to create the next generation of Eagles. Also by June, AMC realized the new 18i was not making it in the market. Price cuts were announced to try to get the new Renault selling.

A rebate of 10 percent of the base price of all Concords, Spirits, Eagles, Renaults and Jeeps was a strong attempt to rekindle the market and lure buyers into the showrooms, but with high unemploy-

In 1981, the Griffith Company offered the Concord and Eagle convertible conversions.

ment and high interest rates, the rebates couldn't change the world. They did serve to get whatever floor traffic there was and helped to keep some dealers in business for a while longer.

Fuel economy was certainly improved over just two years prior. Spirits were rated 23 mpg city /33 mpg highway for the base four-speed four-cylinder combination, while the Concord six with automatic was 19 mpg city/26 mpg highway. The problem was that most of the public couldn't buy a car no matter what it got for fuel mileage, and those that were able to buy generally wanted one of the newer styled front-wheel-drive cars from GM that boasted even better mileage.

Too, AMC missed the boat on a few product points. The biggest missed opportunity was the Eagle Kammback. With its base price of $5995 and fuel economy of 22 mpg city/29 mpg highway, it was a unique item on the American market. It had genuine four-wheel-drive performance, and when equipped with a roof rack, styled wheel covers and driving lights, it had a mini-Cherokee look to it. The price and mileage combination could have overcome many buyers' objections, but the Kammback was never advertised or marketed aggressively, as AMC marketing people were embarrassed to be stuck selling what they considered just a four-wheel-drive Gremlin. All emphasis was given to the sportier SX/4 and the senior Eagles.

Meyers, the man who was given a four-year contract by Renault when it took over 46 percent of the company, was gone from the company by January 1982 and was replaced by Paul Tippett, whose old job as AMC president was taken by over by a senior Renault executive, Jose J. Dedeurwaerder. This was the start of a period of management changes at AMC that left analysts confused.

The final numbers for 1981 give the reader some idea as to market conditions that year. Sales were up slightly, to $2,588,923,000, but unit sales of cars and Jeeps dropped. Based on calendar year wholesale sales, the measure now used at AMC, North American cars dropped from 203,251 to 179,834, while Jeep dropped to 63,216 from 67,312 the prior year. In the overseas markets, cars actually rose to 26,907 from 25,686 while Jeeps also rose, 41,412 versus 31,559. That meant that total unit sales were down to 311,369 from 327,808 in 1980 or 418,204 in 1979. Worse, Jeep sales were still in the gutter, and those were the most profitable sales. Stringent cost cutting, by now an ancient art at AMC, cut the loss quite a bit. American Motors ended up losing "only" a net $136,563,000 for 1981. Working capital, which had been pumped up by Renault, dipped to $164,586,000. That had been a lot of money at one time, but at the rate AMC was able to lose money now, it wasn't nearly enough.

The new top management team predicted a sales upturn for 1982. A term they used to explain their optimism was the "pent-up demand" of a market that had been down very badly for over two years. Industry production of cars in 1981 had dipped even further, to 6.2 million units, the lowest level in more than 15 years. Truck production was less than half of the peak year of 1978, although it was beginning to trend upwards again. The market was just plain lousy.

For 1982, AMC had to again beg its dealers to just hang on for a little while longer. The new joint venture car was being built on a pilot line basis, to try out the tooling, and volume production was planned to begin in June 1982 for a fall introduction. Right now it was fall of 1981, and the 1982 cars, all carryover models, would be all that was on the shelf until then.

David Van Peursem, AMC general manager of marketing, knew he had to concentrate his advertising on product advantages instead of extolling the beauty of the cars themselves. After all, the Concord body was now on the market, in one form or another, for 13 years, so it wasn't something that lit a fire of desire. Still, the design staff had managed to keep the Concord and Spirit very attractive, and with Ziebart Factory Rust Protection, the Buyer Protection Plan, and a 100 percent galvanized steel body, the AMC cars had a strong product message. There was a new five-speed manual gearbox, built by Borg-Warner, offered on all AMC cars. Teamed with the four-cylinder engine, it provided gas mileage of 25 mpg city and a whopping 37 mpg highway. "Fellas," one AMC zone manager asked of his dealers, "did you ever expect to see the day when we'd get 37 miles per gallon from a Concord?" It actually was a remarkable achievement. It was just two years too late.

Still, it was a complete line of cars, from Spirit sedans all the way up to Eagle station wagons, all with fuel economy improvements. Concords got a new two-tone paint option. The Spirit GT package was emphasized. The sales brochures for 1982 are perhaps the nicest catalogs ever put out by the company. Printed on thick, expensive paper, and packed with beautiful pictures, they seem to have come in response to the drab 1981 brochures. There were other changes as well. Select-Drive was now standard on all Eagles. Low drag disc brakes were standard across the board. The warranty was revised to give a second year of coverage for the power train.

Jeep had a new upmarket trim for the CJ-7, a special luxury model called the Limited. It came fitted with wider axles, softer shock absorbers, and leather seat trim, as well as a host of standard equipment items. The Limited was supposed to appeal to the buyer who wanted the luxury of a full-size sport utility in a smaller, more fuel-efficient package. Scrambler was back with some new colors

Top: For 1982, AMC cars were marketed as "the tough Americans." Spirit D/L liftback was stylish. Bottom: All AMC cars now offered optional five-speed transmission. The 1982 Concord D/L wagon is shown here.

Top: 1982 Eagle SX-4 shown with optional aluminum wheels. Bottom: Eagle wagon for 1982 was the most popular Eagle, capable of towing up to 3,000 pounds.

Top: Jeep added the CJ-7 Limited model for 1982, well trimmed but expensive. Bottom: CJ Laredo was a popular package for 1982.

Top: 1982 Jeep Scrambler had classic styling, shown here with optional wood side rails. Bottom: Jeep J-10 Honcho Sportside pickup was an attractive model.

and new options. The Scrambler was a hit, one of the few Jeep had, but even here, the AMC marketing people were having trouble deciding if Scrambler should be marketed as a truck or a sport utility vehicle. Scrambler was being presented as a model in the CJ line instead of a vehicle in its own right. In mid-1980, Jeep started a program called TST for "Time to Sell Trucks," and put extra effort in pushing its J series pickups. But when it came to Scrambler, Jeep didn't sell it as an alternative to imported trucks. With its four-cylinder engine and compact shape, the Scrambler was the only American-made small truck, and if it had been marketed properly, it could have sold in much higher numbers. As it was, it still outsold the imported Subaru Brat and Chevy Luv four-wheel-drives.

The J10 and J20 trucks were offered in a wide array of colors and trim packages for 1982, including Custom, Pioneer, Honcho, and Laredo. The J trucks had first come to market in 1962 as 1963 models, so by 1982 they were very much old hat. Still, they were solid vehicles, and they wore the Jeep name, one that until recently had been almost magical. Likewise, Cherokees for 1982 came in all sorts of trim options that were stunning. The four-door Laredo on the narrow wheel chassis had most of the look of the wide wheel models, but the narrower tires gave much better gas mileage. The Wagoneer line was mostly carryover in the familiar Custom, Brougham, and Limited models offered the year before. Wagoneer's sales had not slumped as badly as Cherokee's. That confused some people, since they were nearly identical vehicles and the Wagoneer was more expensive. The explanation was the market itself. The Cherokee had always been popular with middle-class families, the very folks who were being hurt the worst by the relentless recession. Wagoneers were sold primarily to people of means, and they were not hurt by the recession as much as the common man.

It was a carryover line of vehicles, but one that benefited from various refinements and improvements. A midyear introduction was set for a new Renault product, the Fuego sport coupe. Fuego was based on the 18i chassis but had its own body, a two-door hatchback sporty car that was to compete against the Toyota Celica and other cars of that ilk. The styling was a bit unusual but likable. Sales were planned in the 10,000 range on an annual basis. The LeCar line was expanded at the start of the model year with the addition of a four-door hatchback model. Still hampered by its lack of an automatic transmission, the four-door at least gave the line something new and exciting to show.

With Gerry Meyers gone, it was clear that Renault was tightening its grip on American Motors. As the trade paper, *Automotive News*, stated in a January 1982 article, "While AMC officials proclaimed the alliance was a marriage, there was little doubt that Renault was the head of the household." Roy Chapin was elected by the board of directors to head a new executive committee. This was, perhaps, a dual purpose appointment, for besides his management skill, Chapin also possessed a calm demeanor and self-assurance that Wall Street's analysts and investors found reassuring.

The questions most people wanted answered in 1982 concerned the new X42 small car, for by now it was clear that the new car was the one that would save AMC. Would it be sold as a Renault or an AMC? Or, as some dealers requested, as an AMC-Renault? Would future Concords and Spirits be based on a common chassis shared with the new car? And if the X42 was to be labeled a Renault, what would happen to the AMC line of cars? Would there even be an AMC car in two years? It was the subject of hundreds of conversations across the country, at AMC factories, dealerships, Wall Street, and auto magazines. What would the X42 be branded?

Meyers had been asked that direct question many times in 1981, but he had skirted the issue. It seems to have been a flash point among AMC executives, and almost a recurrence of the decisions made in the fifties to abandon the Hudson and Nash brands. This time more was at stake, for to brand the new car a Renault would not only signal the end of the AMC brand, but the end of the

Top: The Wagoneer Limited for 1982 was an elegant top-of-the-line Jeep. Bottom: Cherokee Laredo wide-wheel from 1982.

Top: 1982 Renault LeCar showed few changes for the two-door model. Bottom: LeCar now came in a four-door model as well. Note conventional door handles.

For 1982, the Eagle showed off new Select-Drive four-wheel drive and gas mileage figures of 23 city/32 highway achieved with a 2.5 liter four and five-speed overdrive transmission.

257

fourth American manufacturer, in name at least. Renault was owner of AMC by just about any measure, but as long as its ownership was less than 50 percent, and there was still an AMC line of cars, folks could reassure themselves that the world was in order. If the X42 was branded a Renault, it would mean that AMC was really nothing more than a French company, and by association, so was Jeep.

Much speculation was also bandied about the new line of downsized vehicles that were to replace the senior Jeeps. This was to be the first redesign of these vehicles since their introduction in late 1962, and the first attempt by AMC. The mainstream Cherokee line was just not coming out of its slump, and the only thing that would revive it was a completely new design that would feature major weight reductions for improved gas mileage. Jeep designers were struggling along, mindful of the necessity of designing a vehicle that would be state of the art in 1983 and still competitive throughout its expected production run of 10 years or more. Meanwhile, a new four-cylinder engine was being tooled. The new engine displaced 2.5 liters, just like the GM engine, but was entirely designed and would be built by AMC. The move to get back into four-cylinder engine building was necessary, as the 2.5 would be the volume engine for the new Jeeps. The cost of designing and tooling for the AMC four-cylinder was fairly high, over $50 million, but would provide a better, less costly engine for what would again be the AMC's most important products.

By May the guessing was over for the X42 as AMC revealed that the new car would be called the Renault Alliance. Marketing Chief Joseph Cappy also revealed that the Spirit and Concord cars would be discontinued before the start of the 1985 model year, and that the Eagle line would eventually be rebadged as Jeeps. Why he chose to describe the end of the AMC brand in so cavalier a fashion, when every AMC dealer was struggling, trying to sell those very cars in a desperately tough market, is anybody's guess. Cappy also bragged that he had increased production of the Fuego by 3,500 units because "it's hard to tell how big it can go."

Excitement grew as the introduction date for the Alliance came nearer. AMC, realizing that this was its only chance to sell its way out of the hole it was in, planned the biggest advertising budget in its history. Van Peursem explained the message would be that "now, for the first time, all these wonderful things associated with European technology are available at an affordable price." In sales training seminars held for dealer personnel, a video tape presentation was shown. In the film, a vague outline of a car is shown driving along, as backround music slowly builds, growing louder and finally becoming a recognizable song based on Neil Diamond's "America." As the dealers and their salesmen sat in the darkened hall listening, perhaps thinking back over the past three and a half years of struggle, remembering the frustrations, the financial reverses, the many good friends who had been forced out of business, the song slowly became louder and clearer ... "We've been waiting for so long ... Now it's coming to America!" Many of the men openly wept.

It was explained to these dealers, the front line troops who had been bloodied in the worst auto market in 50 years, that the Alliance was better than they ever expected, better than anything else on the market. "It's like a quartz digital watch in a wind-up world" is how the announcer explained it. And it was.

It's difficult to explain exactly how advanced the Alliance was for its time. Front-wheel-drive was a popular feature, but many popular Japanese automobiles still did not have it. Alliance did. Fuel injection was a costly feature reserved for only the best cars on the road. Alliance had it. Alliance not only had front disc brakes, it had power-assisted front disc brakes on all models as standard equipment. The standard equipment list also included full carpeting, radial tires, bucket seats, four-speed

Alliance D/L two-door for 1983.

Soon to be the "Car of the Year" - the 1983 Renault Alliance D/L four-door.

overdrive transmission, chrome scuff mouldings, carpeted trunk, oil level and water temperature gauges, trip odometer, and rack and pinion steering. It all came, not on a cheap-looking hatchback, but on a beautiful two-door sedan of the three-box school of design, as handsome a car as you could ask for, and much more attractive than the competition. Priced at $5595, it offered superior value at a surprisingly low price.

It was a good product, and a good thing it was, for the 18i was a flop on the market. The introduction in 1981 had been poorly done, with too big an emphasis on the drab price leaders. Too, the quality of the 18i was poor even for the times, with troubles from thin paint to trim that fell off during test drives, along with numerous electrical problems. The Fuego was selling at a fair clip, but certainly nothing to brag about. The LeCar was the lowest-priced car in the lineup, but the Alliance was sure to be the volume car.

The Alliance was featured on the cover of the 1982 annual report. Actually, the Alliance had been shown on the prior year's cover as well, in a teaser photo that only showed the front end. It also served to show how important the product was for AMC, being featured on the cover for two years in a row. There's no way to overstate it, the entire AMC organization was waiting for the Alliance. It became one of the most important products in AMC history, yet it was not even an AMC car. The launch of the Alliance came off very well, as the dealer force was well trained and pumped up to sell, the factory was building Alliances in quantity and at the right quality from the start, and the product mix at the dealerships was properly balanced. Advertising support was strong with a TV ad schedule that showed a lone Alliance sitting across a gorge. The gorge suddenly closes up, while an announcer states that the Alliance bridges the gap between European quality and American affordability. The dealer body held old-fashioned "by invitation only" introductions of the Alliance where French champagne was served with Wisconsin cheese, symbolic of the two partners.

Still, it couldn't save the company from reporting a loss for the 1982 fiscal year. The Alliance was introduced at the normal fall time, so the 1982 results do show some effect of early wholesale sales to dealers, but also, unfortunately, the high launch costs that were incurred. Sales rose to $2,878,416, but losses also rose to $153,474,000. This meant that, since the highwater mark of 1979, AMC had lost $490,812,000, nearly half a billion dollars. Working capital dropped to $73,795,000. It was a combination of things that had caused the loss. Besides those already mentioned, AMC's subsidiary in Mexico, VAM, suffered a collapse in sales as the Mexican economy slumped. Overseas sales of AMC and Jeep dropped from 68,319 to 31,917, less than half. U.S. sales of cars, at 186,957, and Jeeps at 67,646, were both up a bit, but nowhere near the break-even point. That break-even point was rising year by year as cash was funneled into AMC for the new Renault line and the new Jeep soon to follow.

The Renault Alliance was a smash hit, taking investors' attention away from bad financial news and focusing it instead on product. It wasn't all good news. The 18i reported sales in 1982 of less than 8,000 cars, far less than the 35,000 that Meyers had predicted earlier. The 18i was thus another product flop, and a sore one, for it was one of the most modern cars in the Renault stable, and that company hoped to continue supplying it from their main plant in France. Sales of imported Renaults totaled about 38,000 units, much better than before the tie-up with AMC but certainly not much when the total investment in AMC was considered. Still, it was only the beginning, and now that Alliance was in production, volume should grow.

Motor Trend magazine named the Alliance "Car of the Year" for 1983, the first time AMC won that award since the 1963 Rambler 20 years prior. A lot of water had passed under the bridge in those

Print ad of the 1983 Renault Alliance "Bridging the Gap" between European excellence and affordability evolved into popular TV ad.

261

*From the 1982 annual report, W. Paul Tippet (left) and Jose Dedeurwaerder (right), shown with the 1983 "Car of the Year" trophy from **Motor Trend** magazine.*

20 years, but no team at AMC had been able to repeat the success of George Romney and design chief Ed Anderson.

The 1982 annual report also mentioned that the Spirit and Concord lines were going to be phased out during the 1983 model year to "accommodate production of new passenger cars based on the highly successful Renault Alliance platform." AMC also reported selling one of its three plastics companies, Windsor Plastics, to concentrate on its core business. It was the start of the sell-off of assets that the continuing losses was making unavoidable. Next on the list to go was AM General as it was noted that a buyer was being sought for that major subsidiary. It was a shock, but probably in the best interests of all concerned. Since Renault was now in charge of AMC, and the French government owned Renault, the effect was that American military vehicles were being built by the French government, not a situation that the Pentagon was likely to let stand for long.

Paul Tippet was quoted in *Automotive News* during November 1982 as saying, "For Renault, the purchase of AMC is the deal of the century." His earlier prediction about AMC being able to "take some lumps without getting in the soup" had not proven to be wholly accurate.

By December 1982, the 50,000 Alliances had been built. It was very much the new volume product for AMC, but the Spirit and Concord were still there too, back for one last year in the market. Both cars now came with the 258 cid six-cylinder as standard equipment. The line was heavily pruned and simplified. The Spirit sedan was dropped as was the base liftback. The Spirit D/L was

262

Top: Spirit G.T. became a separate model instead of an option package for 1983. Bottom: 1983 Concord D/L sedan, shown with optional plastic wheelcovers, now came with a 4.2 liter six as its only engine.

Top: 1983 Eagle SX-4 had carryover styling. Bottom: 1983 Eagle wagon was still a popular family car.

Top: 1983 Jeep Wagoneer Limited. Bottom: Macho 1983 Jeep Cherokee wide-wheel Laredo.

still offered, along with the Spirit GT, now a model instead of an option package. The GT equipment included blackout chrome, steel-belted Arriva tires, cast aluminum road wheels, handling package, fog lights, and gauge package, so it now included functional as well as appearance equipage. But AMC underestimated demand, and the car was in short supply when it was introduced.

Concord two-doors were also dropped, so the line consisted of four-door sedans and wagons, in base and D/L trims, along with a single station wagon in the Limited trim. Fuel economy ratings were down because of the loss of the four-cylinder engine, but the Spirit with five-speed was still rated at 21 mpg city/34 mpg highway. That was good for the heavy, six-cylinder rear drive cars they were. The Spirit and Concord stressed their durability and were marketed under the banner "THE TOUGH AMERICANS."

But they couldn't match gas mileage with the Alliance. Almost no one could match that car, for the ratings on it were 37 mpg city/52 mpg highway, the highest rated gas engine cars built in North America.

The Eagle line still had the four-cylinder engine as standard. Midway through the model year, the new AMC 2.5 engine replaced the GM unit. The Eagle line lost the Kammback model, and the two-door sedan in the senior, or 30 series Eagle line, as those two styles went out of production. The rest of the Eagle line was carryover.

The new 2.5 liter engine also began to show up in the Jeep CJ midway through the year. The 1983 Jeep line was mostly carryover, as the company had its plate full with the new Alliance, the new engine, and the soon-to-be-arriving new line of senior Jeeps.

In the early part of the 1980s, the economy began to climb out of the cellar after a long slump. U.S. automobile production hit its lowest point in 1982 when 4.9 million cars were made. Truck production hit its low in 1980 and began a slow climb upwards in 1981. For 1983, U.S. car production bounced back sharply, to 7.1 million units, and trucks came in at 2.4 million, combining to make the best year since 1979. The drought was over, although things were still dicey. The new Alliance hit a home run, selling over 140,000 units. Total wholesale passenger car sales for calendar 1983 were 265,999 for the United States and Canada, up from 186,957 in 1982. Jeeps also rose to 93,169 from 67,646. The slump in overseas sales worsened, dropping to 24,294 from the weak 31,917 of 1982. The total was thus 97,000 more units for 1983, but the only other good news that Tippett and Dedeurwaerder were able to report was that AMC finally had a profitable quarter. The fourth quarter netted $7.4 million in profits. But for the year, it was a loss yet again, $146,730,000. The two leaders reported that 1983 was "one of substantial progress" but that line was starting to wear thin. AM General was sold for $170 million, Wheel Horse Products was sold, and even the American Center, AMC's headquarters building that was the symbol of a resurging AMC in the sunny year of 1979, was sold to raise cash. AMC now became a tenant in its own headquarters.

A worldwide sales goal of 450,000 units was set for 1984, not anywhere near the 600,000 goal once sought. High hopes for good volume and consistent profits rested on the new Jeep and the new passenger car for 1984, a hatchback version of the Alliance badged as the Renault Encore.

The 1984 Jeep Cherokee and Wagoneer were the first all-new line of Jeeps since the 1963 Wagoneer. Unmentioned by the press, these were also the first all-new Jeep products from American Motors. Since AMC purchased Jeep in 1970, 14 years earlier, it had not had to invest in a redesign. AMC's tooling budgets had paid for all-new cars in that time, to no avail. One wonders where Jeep might have gone in the pickup market if the necessary redesign had been funded back in 1974 or 1975. It does no good to dwell on it, for the fact is it just didn't happen.

Top: 1983 Renault 18i sedan. Bottom: 1983 Renault 18i station wagon.

Top: Fuego Turbo for 1983. Bottom: 1983 Renault LeCar.

The 1984 Renault Encore three-door was roomy and attractive.

To the rescue - the 1984 Jeep Wagoneer Limited (foreground) and Jeep Cherokee were the first all-new Jeeps since 1963.

Top: Cherokee Chief was the most popular Jeep Cherokee for 1984. Bottom: Seldom seen, the base model Cherokee four-door.

But these new Jeeps WERE funded, and better still, they were here now, and they looked wonderful. Six inches narrower, 21 inches shorter, and a whopping 1,000 pounds lighter, the new Jeeps offered able performance using just the 2.5 liter four, which was standard equipment. A 2.8 V-6 built by GM was available to those who wanted extra power or greater towing capacity. Part of the weight reduction came from the elimination of the conventional full frame. These new Jeeps were built with a uni-body design made popular by AMC. To provide a large amount of rigidity, needed in an off-road vehicle, a separate frame, thinner than usual, was welded directly to the floor pan. This unique frame/chassis system was called Uni-Frame. Front suspension still utilized a solid front axle for durability but received a complete redesign to provide for a ride as smooth as competing vehicles that used the more fragile independent front suspension. The new Jeep suspension was dubbed Quadra-Link. Transmission choices were four-speed, five-speed, or automatic, while two four-wheel-drive systems -- conventional shift on the fly part-time four-wheel-drive or exclusive Selec-Trac full-time four-wheel-drive -- were offered.

It was a most complete, up-to-date vehicle. Indeed, Quadra-Link, Uni-Frame, and Selec-Trac made it a state-of-the-art set of vehicles, ones that pushed the envelope of four-wheel technology. Quality was good and pricing was competitive. AMC was a bit gun shy in predicting first year expected sales, as the new Jeeps were entering the market after the new and similar Chevy S-10 Blazer, GMC Jimmy, and Ford Bronco II. Initial reports were that AMC planned for 40,000 units combined of the new Cherokee and Wagoneer. By introduction day, the estimate was up to 75,000-80,000.

The rest of the Jeep line was carryover with the usual changes made to rationalize the lineup. Of historic importance was the dropping of the CJ-5 series, as sales of that model had been in the cellar ever since the TV news program, "60 Minutes," alledged that the short wheelbase of the vehicle made it prone to tip over on fast corners or during evasive maneuvers. The CJ-5 had really not been needed in the Jeep line for several years as the CJ-7 was a more versatile and comfortable unit that cost the same to build, gave better interior room, and was long enough to allow an optional automatic transmission. The Wagoneer Limited was renamed the Grand Wagoneer in recognition of its large size, while the Limited name was moved to the top of the new downsized Wagoneer series.

The Eagle line of four-wheel-drive cars was still selling at a fair clip, so they returned for the 1984 model year offered as a four-door sedan in a base series or as a station wagon in base, Limited, or Sport. The average Eagle buyer at this time was considerably better off financially than AMC buyers in the past, and the Eagle was held in high esteem by the public, although it was considered a fairly expensive car for the time. The Eagle SX-4 was dropped along with the Spirit and Concord. The AMC brand was down to just one model in two body styles.

The Alliance was back with only the most minor of detail changes. The promised new small car, the Encore, was a bit of a disapointment as it was clearly just a hatchback version of the Alliance. The two-door was an attractive enough car, but the large, oddly shaped rear hatch window was just too much for the four-door version. It looked very French.

Not withstanding, the new car was certainly a welcome addition, as AMC dealers needed more and more new product to sell. The 18i sedans were dropped, failures in the market, but the 18i wagons were kept on, rebadged as Renault Sportwagons. It was an attempt to be able to supply a station wagon in case any Alliance prospects wanted one. Actually, people visiting the showrooms were beginning to ask for an Alliance wagon, but one was not available yet, so the Sportwagon was pushed instead. Fuegos received some minor freshening, but not enough. A larger 2.2 liter engine

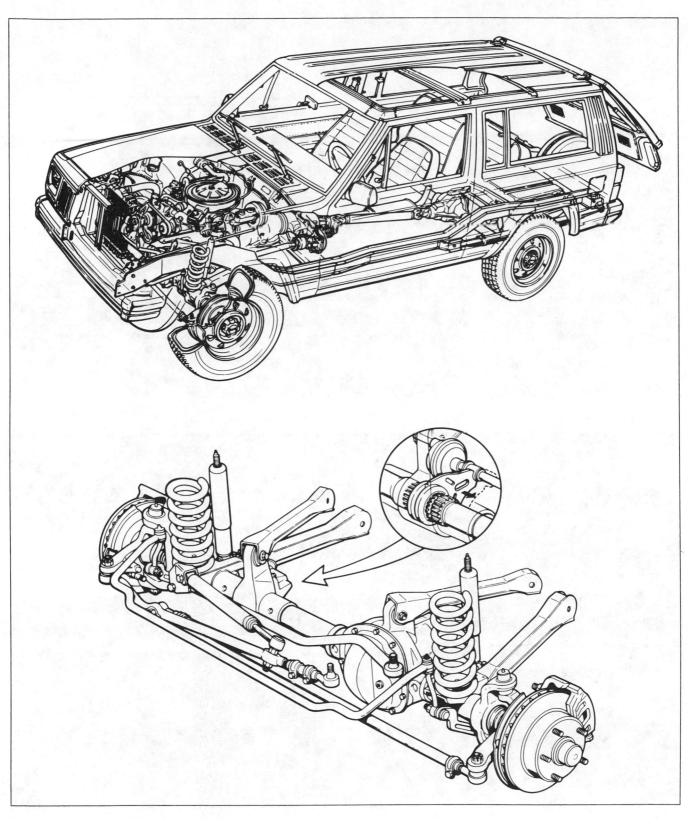

Top: Phantom view of the Cherokee two-door for 1984. Bottom: The 1984 Cherokee/Wagoneer front suspension. Insert shows axle disconnect.

273

For 1984, the Jeep Wagoneer was all new and featured downsized body and plenty of luxury.

Dramatically beautiful, the 1984 Jeep CJ-7 Laredo.

was made standard for non-turbo models to address complaints that the cars were too slow. The Renault LeCar, which had been the first Renault sold by AMC, was dropped. The Encore would now be the lowest-priced car at the AMC agency.

In August 1984, Dick Teague announced his retirement from AMC. Since his hiring by Ed Anderson in 1958, Teague had been responsible for a great number of AMC products, some remarkably modern and evergreen, like the Hornet/Gremlin/Concord/Eagle; some regrettable flops, like the Matador coupe, Marlin, and Pacer.

There was lots of news about AMC itself. A deal was finally agreed on whereby the Republic of China and AMC would jointly build Jeeps for the Chinese market and eventually for export to other Asian markets, including Japan. The new company, named Bejing Jeep, would build the new Cherokees from kits, taking advantage of China's 60 cents per hour wages.

In the United States, one AMC executive was beginning to be noticed as a mover and shaker at AMC. Joseph Cappy, who had let the cat out of the bag about the demise of the Concord and Spirit,

275

Top: Jeep Scrambler for 1984 remained the only convertible top pickup on the market. Bottom: Jeep J-10 pickup for 1984.

The CJ-7 "Special Value Package" sold for $8,813 and was one of several special Jeeps offered in the early 1980s.

Top: For 1984, the Eagle received new standard wheel covers, as shown on this 1984 Eagle four-door. Bottom: Late 1983 Eagles began to have new AMC 2.5 liter engine installed. For 1984, the 2.5 was standard on all Eagles. The 4.2 six was still an option.

Top: 1984 Alliance "L" two-door. Bottom: 1984 Alliance D/L four-door.

1984 Encore four-door had bulbous rear window and odd French styling.

was group vice president of sales and marketing. In one interview he had related that the average AMC buyer was "Mr. and Mrs. Joe Lunch Bucket," a statement that angered the dealer body. Cappy was also quoted as saying he wanted to add a minivan, built in Europe by Matra for Renault, to his U.S. lineup. He revealed that new products coming in the near future included a compact pickup truck built on the Cherokee platform, a vehicle he said "will be a major, major event for us." Another new product from the Alliance chassis was also planned, according to Paul Tippett, but he was coy when asked what it would be. "I don't know yet" he said, "I think it'll be a station wagon. I'll speculate it's a station wagon." That was good news for more and more people coming into AMC showrooms were interested in buying an Alliance station wagon.

The year went better for AMC than the previous four years. Sales volume, pumped by the new high ticket Jeeps and good volume of the Encore/Alliance, hit a new high, $4,215,191,000, as AMC broke the $4 billion mark for the first time. Also, for the first time since 1979, there was a profit, a very slender $15,469,000. Wholesale sales of cars in North America fell to 237,309, but that was offset by a large increase in North American Jeeps, to 171,036. Overseas sales had an increase as well, to a total of 34,038 units wholesale. In recognition of the need to continue to introduce new products, a new intermediate line of cars was planned to be built in a new factory in Brampton, Ontario, Canada, just a few miles from the existing Brampton plant. Unlike that small facility, the new plant would have production capacity of 150,000 units, the number now considered to be a minimum for an auto plant to be profitable.

While it was good to see AMC finally trying to get back into the more profitable intermediate market, it was again being done with an all-new chassis not shared with any other U.S. line, and in a single body style that was supposed to sell in high volume in the hottest segment of the marketplace. It all sounded too much like the Matador coupe all over again.

Chapter 7

1985-1987
Time Runs Out

In the fall of 1984, as the 1985 model year began, AMC seemed at last to be out of the woods. Its Alliance and Encore were two modern entries in the subcompact market. Cherokee/Wagoneer were brand new entries in the hot sport-utility market, and Eagle was getting what there was of a four-wheel-drive passenger car market. AMC as a whole was back into a profit-making position after years of gigantic losses.

But the market was turning again and AMC wasn't prepared for it. All its product planning for cars had been based on ever increasing gasoline prices, a mistake many car companies made. When 1985 came around, gas prices had stabilized at the lowest prices in years. Predictably, the fickle U.S. consumer began shopping for larger cars, ones in the compact and intermediate ranges.

This was excellent news for Jeep, for the new station wagons could skim off a healthy share of those buyers. But it strongly affected sales of the Alliance/Encore series.

Tippett's statement the prior year about a station wagon version of Alliance was a smokescreen, for the new Alliance model was a convertible. This was a fairly expensive way to spend development funds, as even in the best of markets a convertible would never outsell a station wagon. Although the new Alliance convertible was a pert and perky addition to the line, many dealers were disappointed, as buyers were asking for station wagons. The new convertible was based priced at $10,295, making it the lowest-priced convertible on the market.

A 1.7 liter engine was standard on the convertibles and optional on the rest of the line. The engine was a welcome addition; demand was shrinking in the subcompact market as buyers snapped up larger, more powerful cars. The emphasis on good gas mileage, so long a part of the market, was much less important for 1985. Power, room and comfort were what the American consumer wanted this year, not the 1.4 liter gas miser that the Alliance was. At this point, AMC should have dumped

For 1985, the Eagle received a styling update with SX-4 hood and grille.

the 1.7 liter into all Alliance L and D/L models, saving the 1.4 liter for Encore and the base model Alliance, but AMC didn't think fast enough. The market walked away.

The Jeep Cherokee and Wagoneer added a Renault-built turbo-diesel, a 2.1 liter unit that provided world class fuel economy. The list of new features for 1985 included shift-on-the-fly added to the Selec-Trac four-wheel-drive system, rocker/recliner bucket seats, and pop-out rear quarter windows for two-door Cherokees. The new diesel gave fuel economy of 31 mpg city/36 mpg highway when hooked up to the five-speed, an impressive set of numbers. The remainder of the Jeep line was carry-over with only detail changes. The turbo diesel Jeeps generated more press coverage than sales, but they were considered a high tech achievement, and as such were viewed in a positive light.

The Eagle line came in for some important changes and improvements. The 258 cid sixcylinder was made standard equipment, a smart move since the market had turned completely around and no longer wanted a four-cylinder in that size car. The five-speed manual transmission was standard, as was the new shift-on-the-fly feature for four-wheel-drive. A weak attempt at a no-cost restyling was made by using the hood and grille of the old SX/4 model. Wire wheel covers became available. The Eagle line again consisted of a base four-door sedan as well as a wagon in base or Limited models with a Sport Package option for the station wagon only.

The subcompact car market began to weaken in 1984, and by 1985 was shrinking fast. Competition between makers heated up as a fight was waged for market share. Sales of Alliance and Encore sank, while Eagle sales continued the slow downward spiral that had begun in 1983. Fuego and 18i were slow as well, but they had never really amounted to much volume anyway. By April, AMC was again reporting losses, this time a loss of $29 million for the first quarter. Dedeurwaerder reacted by slashing department budgets by 25 percent.

Paul Tippett resigned his full-time position as AMC chairman, staying on as a "part-time chairman" at a reduced salary. Rumors were rampant about the company's future. It was said that Renault was on the verge of selling its share of AMC. That was easy to believe, as changes at Renault in France were bound to impact its U.S. affiliate sooner or later. Bernard Hanon, who had engineered the AMC purchase, had been fired and replaced by Georges Besse. Renault itself had lost over a billion dollars, and Besse was looking at drastic ways to turn things around. One of the things he looked at first was American Motors.

AMC experienced a great deal of labor trouble. An agreement the union had made years before, foregoing wage and benefit increases until 1985, was coming back to haunt AMC. The unions demanded to be paid for the wage increases withheld by AMC back when it seemed that the Alliance, then a year away from production, would ensure enough profits to pay back workers with interest. With the subcompact market now soft, AMC just didn't have the money to honor its promises. The Kenosha, Wisconsin workers were willing to negotiate, despite feeling betrayed by AMC's decision to build its new intermediate car plant in Canada. They had little choice.

Jeep workers in Toledo reacted by sabotaging new Jeeps on the assembly lines. The move pitted labor against management in a classic confrontation that seemed better situated to Detroit of the 1930s rather than Ohio in the 1980s, but there it was. AMC filed suit against the UAW for $300,000 of damages to vehicles.

Future plans were discussed openly. A new compact car, built in France, was to augment the line in 1987. The ultra high performance Renault Alpine would definitely be added to the car line in 1986. The minivan was coming. The new intermediate sedan would debut for the 1988 model year, with a stylish coupe added the following year.

There was even talk that the Kenosha plant would be shut down, and all cars sourced from either the new Canadian plant or from France. Even more fantastic talk was that Chrysler might sign a contract to have AMC assemble its aging but popular "M" body intermediate cars.

What was true was that the Jeep CJ line was being moved again, back to Brampton. With the new Jeeps selling well and a new Cherokee-based pickup truck coming for 1986, room was needed at the Toledo plant, so the tiny Brampton plant was again retooled.

By the end of the year, Paul Tippett faded away, replaced as chairman of the board by Pierre Semerena. With Dedeurwaerder as president, it meant the French were fully in charge now. Joseph Cappy was kept on as executive vice president and chief operating officer. It was another year of disappointment, for the company did not recover in the second half, instead reporting a full year loss of $125.3 million. It was a bitter pill to swallow, but the losses were traceable to the Alliance and Encore and the sales collapse of the subcompact market. Sales of the new Jeeps had improved over the strong showing of 1984, and retail Jeep sales for the United States and Canada came in at 192,835, setting a new record. Total sales volume for AMC was $4,039,901, down four percent from 1984. Wholesale unit sales of cars fell like a stone, down to 136,989 for the United States and Canada, while wholesale Jeep orders came in at 217,806. In the overseas markets, 14,492 cars and 22,482 Jeeps were wholesaled. Both of these were up, but cars more so than Jeep, surprisingly enough. The wholesale total of 391,769 worldwide was thus down 50,614 units, and that was where the profit (or loss) was. In a now tiring refrain, the theme of the annual report was again the future. "Meeting the Challenges of the Next Century" was the statement on the cover, while inside were views of the new products coming soon. It was noted that the stockholders' equity in American Motors now stood at $149 million, down from the $279 million of 1984. 1985 was a wash-out year, but the future was supposedly bright.

Jose Dedurwaerder was interviewed in December 1985 by *Wards Auto World* for a feature article, "1986 State of the Industry." He acknowledged the market shift away from his U.S.-built Renaults, and the length of time before any new volume cars would be coming from AMC. "It's going to be a tough year for us next year, there's no doubt," he said.

He also dropped a bombshell by declaring that AMC would need an all-new assembly plant to replace the Kenosha complex when the Alliance/Encore series came to the end of their product life cycle in 1989. An all-new Alliance/Encore was going to be needed, and Dedeuwaerder wanted a new plant to build it in as well. He felt that the old Kenosha plant, being a multi-storied building, could never be cost competitive with the new single-level plants being built by the Japanese transplants. Too, many states were offering millions of dollars in aid and incentives to the Japanese to entice them into building a plant in their state, while the traditional Big Three and little AMC were left to their own resources. Dedeurwaerder now wanted an incentive deal like the Japanese were being offered.

The 1986 cars were little changed, just as Dedeuwaerder had said. The Alliance/Encore had a sleek new grille with smaller headlamps, and that was about it. The AMC Eagle was back again, although the AMC nameplate had been deemphasized the year before. Tinted glass was added to the standard equipment list, and that was the biggest change.

Jeep had bigger news as the new Comanche pickup truck, based on the Cherokee, debuted. Comanche was offered in both four-wheel-drive or two-wheel-drive, and thus opened up a whole new market for Jeep. The pickup market was booming, and Jeep had not marketed the Scrambler as well as it could have. The Comanche was more a mainstream product, and since it came in both two-

A CONTINUING COMMITMENT TO EXCELLENCE AND INNOVATION.

This fall we will introduce the Jeep Comanche, an exciting new compact pickup. It will offer quality features we believe will surpass all the competition.

Already on the drawing boards are more exciting and innovative products. All of them designed with the needs of you, the consumer, foremost in mind.

We welcome comparison. In fact we thrive on it. That's how our Renault/Jeep partnership got to be the world's fifth largest automaker.

We want you to choose our cars and vehicles. We must in turn give you the reasons to make this choice. You have my personal pledge that today and tomorrow, we will continue to be there with the best.

Jose J. Dedeurwaerder
President & Chief Executive Officer
American Motors Corporation

15

Advertising took on an institutional look as Jose Dedeurwaerder began to appear in a few ads.

286

or four-wheel-drive models, was planned for high volume.

CJ-7 production ended in January 1986 as the Brampton plant was tooled to build its replacement, the all-new Wrangler. Wrangler was a bit hard to figure, for to the casual eye it appeared to be a CJ with square headlamps and nothing more. But Wrangler was designed to cure many nagging difficulties that the CJ had acquired, mainly and firstly, high insurance rates due to the adverse publicity caused by the "60 Minutes" rollover story. Additionally, Wrangler featured a more car-like dashboard, a smoother ride achieved by using elements of the Cherokee suspension, and a much sturdier roll cage construction for safety. AMC emphasized that Wrangler was all-new and shared no components with its predecessor, but it did indeed use the same AMC 2.5 and 4.2 liter engines. Sales goals for the Wrangler were strangely modest, just 30,000 units, the same as the CJ had sold. Why AMC bothered to retool a line without planning to increase its sales is a puzzle, but a minor one.

Midway through 1986, Dedeurwaerder was replaced as president by Joseph Cappy. Car sales for the year were plainly awful, even by AMC standards. Worldwide wholesale car sales dropped to 66,372. Worldwide wholesale Jeep deliveries were 221,362. The total of 287,734 cars and Jeeps was down over 100,000 units from the prior year. It couldn't last.

The loss for 1986 was bad but not as bad as had been expected. The net loss came in at $91,319,000 on sales of $3,486,472. Sales were down over a half billion dollars, yet the loss had been less than the year prior. The budget cuts and better sales mix were having a positive effect, but it was simply too late to do anything to change the course that history now had to take.

Also in mid-1986, Chrysler Corporation, experiencing a sales explosion and running short of production capacity, approached AMC. A deal was proposed wherein AMC would build, under contract with Chrysler, the midsize Chrysler Fifth Avenue, Dodge Diplomat and Plymouth Gran Fury. Chrysler had planned to end production of these cars and replace them with new front-drive models. But the old Chryslers, the "M" bodies is what they were known as, proved to be still popular and sellable. Chrysler wanted to use the old Kenosha plant to build the "M" cars for as long as they remained popular, which of course would help AMC earn some badly needed cash. It was a very unorthodox plan, but not completely without precedent. In the history of American automaking it had been done before, but it was certainly not the usual state of affairs.

For AMC it was as good a deal as they were going to get, and at least it would put some of the dormant production capacity at Kenosha to work, hopefully bringing in profits. In some ways, it was a great deal, for at least AMC only had to build cars, not sell them as well. It did show up, although no one noticed it, one weakness in the AMC product line. Since the Concord had been dropped at the end of 1983, AMC no longer had a conventional family car to offer the public.

Right now the market was hot for midsize, rear-wheel-drive American cars, and the Concord, with its 108-inch wheelbase, now fit into that category. American Motors would be building midsize cars for its competitor, but because the Concord had been dropped, AMC itself had no such car to offer its own customers. It was too bad that the powers in charge at AMC had chosen to bet the fate of the company solely on the Alliance.

Of course, by 1986 it was obvious that such reliance was a mistake. Joe Cappy spoke now of the need for a full line of new cars, but what he meant was Renault, not AMC, cars. The U.S. auto industry had a slight downturn in production for 1986, partly offset by a small increase in trucks built. But AMC got hammered.

For 1987, an attempt was made to enlarge the range of cars offered by cobbling up a new series, the Renault GTA. Created by stuffing a high-performance two-liter engine into the Alliance, GTA

Compare the new two-wheel drive Jeep Comanche to Ford Ranger and Chevy S-10, and you'll find Comanche has the lowest price tag. And in 4x4's, Comanche is the lowest-priced long-bed pickup you can buy.*

Up front, a gutsy 117 horsepower 2.5 litre electronic fuel-injected engine is standard. It's more powerful than the base engine of any other pickup in its class.

Comanche's 119.9 inch wheelbase is longer than any other long-bed pickup in its class.

Comanche is the only 4x4 pickup built with a choice of two "shift-on-the-fly" four-wheel drive systems.

You'll find big 15-inch wheels and all-weather radials standard on Comanche, optional on two-wheel drive Ford Ranger and Chevy S-10.

Four Wheeler of the Year.

Safety belts save lives.

*Based on manufacturers' suggested retail prices for base long-bed vehicles. Excluding taxes, license, destination charges and optional equipment. Prices may change without notice.

Easy to be a truck. Hard to be a Jeep.

New Jeep Comanche
Available in 2WD and 4WD

For 1986, Jeep introduced the new Comanche pickup.

was to compete with the highly successful Volkswagen GTi, Ford Escort GT, and Dodge Omni GLH. GTA came in two-door sedan and convertible styles, both unusual body types in that niche, and had bold body cladding and monochromatic color schemes. If AMC hadn't reacquired its image as a loser, the GTA could have been a solid entry. As it was, sales were only moderate.

Sales of Encore had slipped badly in 1986, so that nameplate was dumped for 1987. Encores were now dubbed "Alliance hatchback," and the only mechanical change was the switch to the center badge Alliance grille.

Jeep introduced its new 4.0 liter in-line six-cylinder engine. Based on the block of the old AMC six-cylinder, the new 4.0 liter was a wizard that put out 173 horsepower and 220 lbs./ft. of torque. Jeep Comanches equipped with the new engine could run 0-60 in 9.5 seconds. The new engine cost less than the old 2.8 V-6 that GM had been supplying, yet gave 50 percent more power and allowed a 5,000-pound towing capacity. The enthusiast press loved it. Offered in Cherokee, Comanche and Wagoneer, it quickly became the engine of choice for most Jeep buyers. A new four-speed automatic transmission from Aisin Seiki of Japan delivered smooth performance and even better gas mileage than before, despite the increase in power. Besides the new engine, Jeep had a new short bed version of the Comanche, as well as tweaks to the rest of the line.

Perhaps it was good business planning, perhaps it was just luck, but the 4.0 liter engine was exactly what Jeep needed to begin to gain back market share. Use of the 4.0 liter also significantly increased AMC's profit potential, for it meant the most expensive component of its only volume product was being built in-house where the profits could enhance the corporate bottom line.

The Eagle was back again for 1987 with the same two body styles, same old-fashioned look, and no real changes to speak of. The sales brochure for that year carries a cover photo of a lone Eagle motoring down a series of rolling hills, with a sunset in the distance. It is a sad tableau, for it was plain that the Eagle's days were numbered. The AMC nameplate was not mentioned as if the Eagle was now its own separate line of cars. It had been planned that this would be the way to slowly change it from an AMC-branded car to a Jeep-branded car, but no one expected the Eagle to be in production long enough to ever wear the Jeep badge. When product plans were talked of in public, plans for Eagles beyond 1988 were not mentioned. It was now becoming more certain that even most of the Renault products were going to be built in Europe, as the money to retool for production in America just wasn't available, either in the United States or from Renault in France.

The dealer body was overstocked with cars and trucks in late 1986, so a radical new incentive was used, "zero percent" financing on all new Jeeps, Eagles and Renaults.

Behind the scenes, unknown to most people in the industry, Lee Iacocca of Chrysler had authorized initial inquiries about a possible buyout of Renault's share of AMC. Iacocca was awash in cash from the unusual success his company was enjoying and thought he spotted a bargain in AMC. As negotiations were progressing, Georges Besse, chairman of Renault and a man who was decidedly interested in removing the loss-plagued AMC from his corporate charts, was gunned down outside his home in Paris, killed by terrorists simply because of his position as a leading capitalist in Europe. The negotiations stalled after that, but the press was still mostly in the dark anyway, with only rumors to go on.

Chrysler was interested in having its aging Dodge Omni and Plymouth Horizon subcompacts built in Kenosha, since they had been replaced by the new P-cars, Sundance and Shadow. Unlike AMC, Chrysler subcompacts were bouncing back in the market, and there were still thousands of customers interested in the Omni/Horizon.

Final color catalog for the Eagle was for the 1987 Eagle.

By March 1987, the news finally broke. Chrysler was indeed going to buy AMC. *Time* magazine called it "A Daredevil Wheel Deal." In a very complete and well written article, *Time's* George Russell noted that the buyout deal had been code-named "Project Titan" by the Chrysler people. Iacocca was quoted as saying, "(The merger) will strengthen both of us in what's already become a tough market." The deal was announced the same month that the newest Renault import, the compact Medallion, was launched on the U.S. market. Medallion thus got a poor send-off, overshadowed by the buyout, but it was so similar to the earlier Renault 18i that it probably would not have sold well anyway.

It was curious timing for Renault to sell now, for it was almost a certainty that AMC was going to be profitable for 1987. A combination of the lower costs of using the new 4.0 liter engine, contract concessions from the unions, profitable Chrysler production in Kenosha, and strong sales of the highly profitable Jeeps meant that AMC really was on the comeback trail for 1987.

Some thought Iacocca was making the mistake of his life. Standard and Poors announced that it was putting Chrysler credit rating on its watch list, with "negative implications." Iacocca himself explained it best in his book "Talking Straight" when he wrote that the assets he most coveted at AMC were its 1,400 dealers, its Jeep line, and the new Bramalea factory, fully built and currently producing the pilot line models of the all-new intermediate car. Renault Premier, the latest car that AMC was pinning all its hopes on, was a very nice car, no question about that, but as one analyst noted, the world wasn't holding its breath waiting for AMC to introduce a new intermediate car. There was plenty of competition out there.

A color picture on the cover of the Aug. 10, 1987 issue of the *Automotive News* showed a waving Lee Iacocca being driven to a stockholders meeting in a World War II vintage Jeep by none other than Joe Cappy, to announce that the deal to buy AMC was done. It had been achieved by offering to pay $4.50 per share, which meant a total purchase price of $1.1 billion. In addition, Chrysler agreed to buy a minimum dollar amount of Renault parts and components over a five-year period for use in the new Premier, or pay a fine for failing to. The negotiations had been kept under wraps at AMC since the summer of 1986. By the first quarter of 1987, when the 1986 annual report was being readied for print, it was considered such a sure deal that the annual report was never actually printed. Thus, the 1985 annual report was the last one for American Motors. A Form 10K report for 1986 does exist, and it shows a profit for the final quarter of the year, which leads one to believe that a full-year profit for 1987 was possible. It was too bad for Renault that it bailed out just when it was going to start earning back its investment. It was, as one AMC board member put it, "as if after nine months Renault decided it didn't really want to be pregnant."

Car sales were lousy again. Alliance retail sales for 1987 were a mere 24,770. The old Eagle retailed 4,564 units in the United States while 192 units of the new Premier were sold. For this final full year of sales, wholesale numbers are not available, as the AMC/Jeep and Renault totals were mixed in with Chrysler figures.

By fall, the entire AMC and Renault car line was renamed Eagle, and American Motors itself became the Jeep/Eagle division of Chrysler Corporation. Because of the mid-year signing of the buy out, some of the old cars would continue in production until things could be sorted out.

And so we come to the end of the line, the 1988 lineup of cars from the Jeep/Eagle division. Surprisingly, the Eagle station wagon was returned, now in its ninth year on the market and still wearing the same body that had debuted in fall of 1969, 19 years ago, as the car that was replacing the Rambler. For 1988, most of the previously optional equipment for Eagle, such as air conditioning, automatic transmission, tilt wheel, etc., was standardized in a move to use up existing stocks of parts quicker, while also making assembly easier by limiting the variations in equipment levels.

The Renault Medallion was rebadged as the Eagle Medallion, while the new Premier was similarly rebadged. Some Premiers were rebadged after they had left the assembly line. Chrysler looked at the upcoming two-door version of the Premier, to be called the Allure, and cancelled it. The Alliance was sold until all dealer stocks ran out and was also cancelled. The Renault Sportwagon was dropped. The Renault minivan and the Alpine sports car never made it across the ocean to America. Chrysler had no use for them.

The Jeep J-10 and J-20 pickup trucks, which had been first shown to the public in 1963, were dropped from production. And finally, after being on the market since 1980 with a body style that dated back to the fall of 1969, production of the Eagle station wagon, last of the cars that can be considered AMC models, ended on Dec. 14, 1987. It was the last model of the last series of the last independent.

Chapter 8

What Went Wrong

What went wrong? Why did American Motors fail? Contemporary writers and historians have always been quick to drag out the tired line that AMC's demise was proof positive that it is impossible for an independent automobile maker to survive in the American market.

That is utter nonsense.

What has been proved by all this is that an independent automaker could survive and prosper in the American market if it was willing to do things differently from its big competitors. George Mason realized in the 1940s that the market was going to get very difficult for the smaller makers, and he set about to join forces with other small makers in order to survive. But Mason's basic plan, while way ahead of anything else being done at the time, was flawed by his basic premise that he could challenge the Big Three in the mass market. If AMC had stuck to his original plan to introduce an all-new line of full-size cars, it would have had its head handed to it on a platter in 1958, during the Eisenhower recession, or in 1959 and 1960 when Ford and Chevy kept restyling their big cars in an all-out battle for market supremacy.

George Romney figured out the way to go was not a frontal attack but rather to outflank the competition by offering something that they didn't have, a midsize or intermediate-size car like the all-new 1956 Rambler. Luckily, Ed Anderson's design was a well-conceived car that appealed to a large group of Americans satisfied with its room and comfort and enamored of its compact dimensions and low operating costs. This basic chassis was used for seven model years, saving millions of dollars in tooling costs, ensuring handsome profits for AMC. Fate and luck teamed up small car apostle Romney with America's foremost compact car designer in a moment that altered the assumed course of history.

Romney also came to realize that an independent could survive on lower sales volumes than the Big Three if it was careful and extremely clever with its tooling costs. Running through the entire history of American Motors is the theme of tooling costs ... when they were carefully spent on well-designed cars, AMC did well. When tooling dollars were wasted on poorly designed cars or expen-

1955 Rambler Country Club hardtop. Note the open front fenders, enclosed rear fenders, elaborate hood ornament and continental spare.

Metropolitan convertible. The Met certainly predicted the future - small, four-cylinder cars built by joint ventures to sell in vast American markets.

Design rendering by Bill Reddig for late '50s Rambler.

sive model programs, the bottom line suffered. Unfortunately, when the bottom line suffered, the press, ever hungry for a story, would begin another round of doom and gloom stories of how it was impossible for an independent to survive. For that reason alone it was crucial for AMC to make few mistakes.

Romney was sure of his belief in extreme caution in tooling investments. It allowed him to override conventional thinking and reintroduce the 100-inch wheelbase car as the Rambler American in 1958, two years after it had been discontinued. For almost no expense he was able to offer the American as a lower-price companion model, one that was bought by thousands of customers. When he did finally order a restyling of that car, it was an extremely clever reskinning of the outer body panels that saved the company millions of dollars, yet still set a sales record. By 1962 Romney had two distinct lines of cars built on two chassis that had been in production for years, spreading amortization expense over many thousands of cars and adding more profits to the company. Forget any ideas that this was a fluke. In 1963 American Motors had its sixth straight year of profits, set a new sales record for an independent which has yet to be beaten, and was readying its all-new 1964 American. AMC was a success that was recognized by the press and the dealers. Rambler cars were very well thought of in the marketplace, evidenced by their continuing strong sales, and the future held not a

295

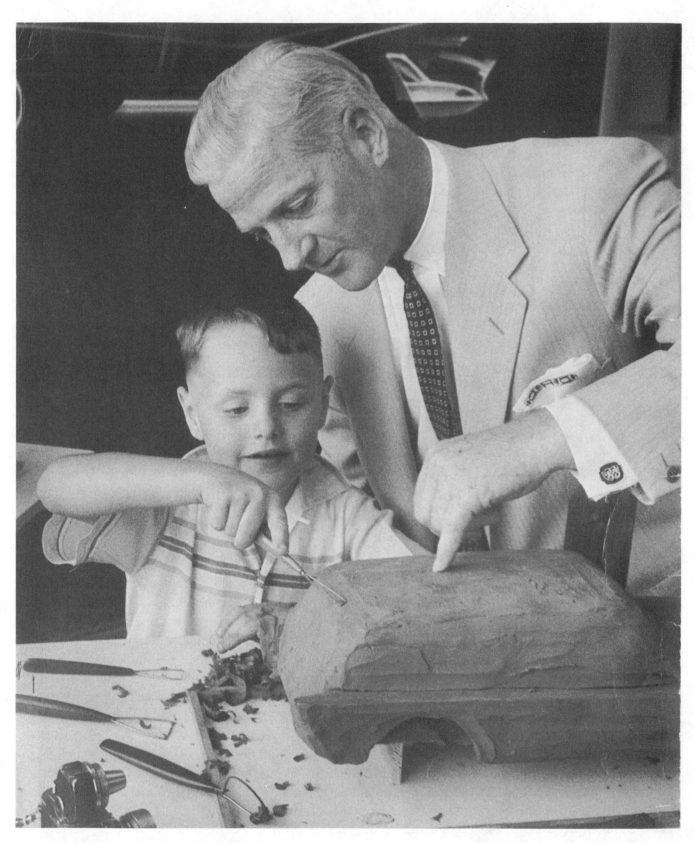

Ed Anderson and a young friend in happier times.

storm cloud in sight. New machinery had been bought and put into place that would allow even greater production at lower costs, either to serve the American market's strong growth or to send to the Latin American markets that were enthusiastic buyers of Ramblers. American Motors was not heading for failure at the beginning of 1963.

The management change which took place meant that the carefully laid plans would be chucked out the window, replaced by the determined dreams of a man who believed he could turn AMC into a full-line automaker, able to design, engineer and produce a full-sized car that would win buyers away from the companies that had been building such cars for so many years. The very people who had already forced Studebaker, Willys, Kaiser, Packard, Graham, Auburn, Frazer, and hundreds of others out of the car business were somehow going to relinquish market share to Roy Abernethy and American Motors, or at least he seemed to think so.

The first move, adding the V-8 engine to the Classic line, seemed to increase sales, yet in reality it began to unravel the carefully woven fabric of AMC's image in the market. The new Marlin that appeared the following year, 1965, further eroded the image of Rambler as a common sense car, while at the same time it wasted millions of dollars of tooling costs and advertising expense on a vehicle that just wouldn't sell. Certainly, the advertising theme of 1965 and 1966 was way out of character for Rambler, failing to attract as many new customers as it was losing of old customers. While millions of dollars were spent to design and merchandise the big new Ambassador, sales of the mainline Classics and Americans sank. Worse of all, tooling costs for the new Ambassador, as well as the new convertibles, put too much debt onto AMC in too short a time. They failed to sell in sufficient volume, causing a drastically reduced profit in 1966, and a huge loss for 1967. In the short span from 1964 to 1966, AMC was crippled, doomed to struggle on with the stench of failure around it, while an eager press waited for the next indication of trouble.

The new cars brought out in 1968, AMX and Javelin, were a step in the right direction. The Gremlin/Hornet program was a better move, sharing a common chassis. But all of these cars failed to bring in the combination of sales volume and high profit margins that the old Rambler Classic had done. That could be considered a failing of AMC management as well, that they never seemed to be able to focus on bringing out a high margin, high volume car after the Rambler Classic was run into the ground.

Roy Chapin's decision to buy Jeep shines on in history as one of the rightest of right moves, and in a way Jeep served as that line of high-margin vehicles. But the 1971 Javelin and AMX were a complete waste of tooling dollars, saddling AMC with still more debt and very few sales. When the Hornet line was expanded, first in 1971 with the Sportabout, then in 1973 with the hatchback, it seemed that the correct path had been found again, a way to increase unit sales without a concurrent big hit on the bottom line. The Hornet chassis should have been used as the foundation for a new Javelin, AMX, and Pacer. A new downsized chassis should have been designed for the Ambassador and Matador to share. Such a program would have returned AMC to the winning formula set out years earlier by George Romney.

It seemed that every time AMC started to get healthy and prosperous, a new attempt would be made to expand the number of chassis and wheelbases used. Witness the 1965 Ambassador, which had its own body and wheelbase, separate from, although admittedly heavily based on, the Classic. When Abernethy was proudly touting that Rambler now came in three distinct sizes, he really felt that it was an advantage. But history has now shown that this program only increased AMC's debt burden, not its sales. Even then, 1964-1965 had not generated a loss, only missed profits and opportunity. That was how strong AMC was in the market. Instead of a pause in investment, AMC continued to restyle and retool its big cars, on separate wheelbases, instead of consolidating back to the one shared chassis and body, such as the 1963 cars had done. The results were predictable ... increased spending combined with decreased sales equaled losses for 1966 and 1967.

When AMC finally regained its balance and began again to generate decent profits, in 1972 and 1973, it managed to do so because of the low costs of the shared tooling for Gremlin and Hornet. But it again decided to expand its chassis offerings by tooling for the all-new 1974 Matador coupe, one of the most expensive projects it ever undertook. The Matador coupe drained the tooling budget and generated sales that can be summed up easily ... lousy. By designing the new Matador as a coupe only, the sedan and station wagon Matador line was doomed to extinction as were the high profit margins that should have been generated from that series. Do not for one instant think that the Matador coupe sold in any sort of volume, for sales results prove it was one of the worst-selling cars in AMC history. If a new downsized body had been introduced that combined the Ambassador and Matador series into one common wheelbase and body, the savings in tooling alone would have made it much more successful than the Matador coupe.

But AMC still didn't learn its lesson. It bounced into 1975 with the Pacer, another all-new chassis with a unique body that could not be built in anything other than two-door models. Overweight right from the start, the Pacer's high per piece amortization schedule and lack of flexibility in model range made it another low-profit, cash-draining product with no future.

To weary eyes, the "dark days of 1967" came back reincarnated and fully rejuvenated as the dark days of 1977. At least Jeep was part of the company in 1977, to help bail out the passenger car division.

Now with all its cash gone, its new Matador and Pacer models fully recognized as failures, AMC was forced to go back to its roots, the common chassis program planned so long ago by George Romney. By 1979 the AMC line was comprised of the Spirit in two body styles, the Concord in four body styles, and a new Eagle to come out in the fall. The whole AMC line of cars was to be based on just one chassis in two wheelbases, saving considerable cost and finally launching AMC back on the path to consistent profits. It would have, too, if only the gas crisis hadn't come along just then to kill any hope of business bouncing back.

The gas crisis and resulting economic downturn in 1979 was enough to finish AMC, but don't blame it on the gas crisis alone. The blame should be placed squarely on the shoulders of management for squandering AMC's future on the ill-conceived Matador coupe and the Pacer.

And now we come to "if only." If only the Matador program had been similar to the concurrent Ford Granada and Mercury Monarch, AMC would have had a high-volume/high-profit car on its hands. If only the Pacer had been based on a 100-inch wheelbase version of the Gremlin chassis, and the $60 million wasted on it instead spent on a new line of Jeeps. If only AMC had come out with its own four-cylinder engine for the Gremlin and Jeep CJ in 1974, instead of 1977 for the Gremlin and 1980 for the Jeep. If only AMC had come out with a restyled Gremlin and Hornet in 1976. If only the gas crisis had come in 1981 instead of 1979 when AMC was too weak to withstand it.

More to the point, if only AMC had stayed on the course set in 1963. If only it had stayed clear of the Marlin and not spent tooling dollars unnecessarily on making the Ambassador bigger than the Classic. If only it had not wasted precious cash tooling for convertibles in 1966. If only it had admitted that the Marlin was a flop and not spent another pile of money in 1967 to retool it on the Ambassador chassis. If only it had only remembered the things that had made it a success in the first place.

AMC cars in better times: the 1960 Ambassadors.

299

As it was, by 1983 it was all over. When the Concord and Spirit were allowed to fizzle out, it was certain that the AMC nameplate was going to be allowed to fizzle out, too. It's almost funny when you consider it. AMC overspent itself by over-expanding its model lineup, but when it finally got itself consolidated to one chassis, it flat out refused to ever restyle it. It had taken years to get back to where it had started, a shared chassis. Yet when it was achieved, the company could not or would not take advantage of it.

By 1983, Renault was its masters voice, and Renault was only interested in Renault brand cars. The ensuing years of struggle show how costly the industry had gotten. It also showed further proof of the wisdom of not expanding to too many platforms. By 1987, AMC had plans to sell the Alliance, Medallion, minivan, Alpine, Eagle station wagon, and Premier all on separate platforms. It was an ambitious but foolhardy program, one that spread marketing dollars too thinly. Although AMC broke into profitabilty in the fourth quarter of 1986, how long would the car division have lasted? It's certain that the Medallion would have flopped on the market, and history has shown that the Premier did not have staying power, either. The minivan never made it to America, as it would have been priced much higher than the competition.

By the mid-1980s, the AMC nameplate was finished in the market, just as the Rambler name and heritage had been wasted in an earlier decade. AMC came to the dark days of 1987.

As a people, we are poorer by the loss of American Motors. Not so much because we will never buy an AMC car, but rather because we no longer have the option of buying an AMC car. Our choice in the market is now that much less. The old line independent automakers have been replaced now by a new generation of multi-nationals with Japanese names, and if truth be told, they are very fine cars. What they lack is personality and eccentricity, and yes, heritage and history.

The old Kenosha, Wisconsin AMC plant was demolished by Chrysler in 1989. (Photo by Larry Mishkar)

The old Kenosha auto plant -- home of the Thomas B. Jeffery Company, maker of Rambler cars; home to Nash, builder of Hudsons; assembly point for AMC and Eagle cars -- is gone now, demolished in 1989 by Chrysler. The Brampton plant is closed. Bramalea now builds the Chrysler LH cars. An all-new Jeep plant was erected in Detroit to build the new Grand Cherokee, and Toledo still builds the old Cherokee. Dick Teague died in May 1991 of cancer. Ed Anderson lived 30 years in the villa he bought in Mexico when he left Detroit that cold winter in 1962, and he now lives in New Orleans. George Romney and Roy Chapin both retired in Michigan. God bless them all, they are wonderful people.

Make no mistake about it. Like the California condor or the dodo bird, the American independent automakers were a rare breed, and when they died a part of our heritage died with them. Like all rare species, once they are gone, they are gone for good, never to return.

1971 Gremlin.

Bibliography

The Story of George Romney, by Tom Mahoney
Standard Catalog of American Cars 1946-1975, John Gunnell, Editor
Standard Catalog of American Cars 1976-1986, James Flammang, Editor
Standard Catalog of American Light-Duty Trucks, John Gunnell, Editor
The American Motors Family Album, 1969 Edition, by John A. Conde
The American Motors Family Album, 1976 Edition, by John A. Conde
Time magazine, various issues
Automotive News, various issues
Wards Auto World, various issues
Car and Driver magazine, various issues
Motor Trend magazine, various issues
Annual Report to the Stockholders of American Motors, 1954 through 1985 editions
Road Test magazine, various issues
Road & Track magazine, various issues
Canadian Cars 1946-1984, by R. Perry Zavitz
Talking Straight, by Lee Iacocca
Annual Report to the Stockholders of Chrysler Corporation, 1987 and 1988 editions
Small Cars magazine, various issues
Official Specifications 1902-1963 Rambler and its Predecessors, by John A. Conde

(Photo by W. Scott Cameron)

About the Author

Although this is Patrick Foster's first book, many readers will recognize his byline from various old-car related magazines for which he has written over the last few years.

Pat's forte has always been AMC-related topics, and he brings his skill and talent to full use in *American Motors, The Last Independent.*

Born in Burlington, Vermont, Pat grew up in the town of Milford, Connecticut. He lives there today with his wife, Diane, and daughter Caitlin. A devoted researcher of lesser known automotive brands, he's a member of the Society of Automotive Historians and is an avid car collector with an admitted soft spot for Ramblers.

2/94